"十二五"国家重点出版规划项目

总主编　刘世铸

ESP
综合英语教程：读写分册1

主　编　谢　楠　王晓军
副主编　廉玲玲　徐钱立　苗纪美
编　者　赵兰凤　高　原　邵珠峰　杨文君

北京大学出版社
PEKING UNIVERSITY PRESS

图书在版编目(CIP)数据

ESP综合英语教程.读写分册.1/谢楠,王晓军主编.—北京:北京大学出版社,2014.1
ISBN 978-7-301-23677-2

Ⅰ.E… Ⅱ.①谢… ②王… Ⅲ.①英语—阅读教学—高等学校—教材 ②英语—写作—高等学校—教材 Ⅳ.H31

中国版本图书馆CIP数据核字(2014)第001385号

书　　　名：	ESP综合英语教程：读写分册1
著作责任者：	谢　楠　王晓军　主编
责 任 编 辑：	刘　强
标 准 书 号：	ISBN 978-7-301-23677-2/H·3462
出 版 发 行：	北京大学出版社
地　　　址：	北京市海淀区成府路205号　100871
网　　　址：	http://www.pup.cn　新浪官方微博:@北京大学出版社
电　　　话：	邮购部 62752015　发行部 62750672　编辑部 62754149　出版部 62754962
电 子 信 箱：	zpup@pup.pku.edu.cn
印 刷 者：	北京宏伟双华印刷有限公司
经 销 者：	新华书店
	787毫米×1092毫米　16开本　7.75印张　220千字
	2014年1月第1版　2020年7月第3次印刷
定　　　价：	32.00元

未经许可,不得以任何方式复制或抄袭本书之部分或全部内容。
版权所有,侵权必究
举报电话:010-62752024　电子信箱:fd@pup.pku.edu.cn

前　言

自1985年我国第一份《大学英语教学大纲》制定以来，大学英语教学已走过20多年的路程，历经三次重大改革。如今，大学英语教学已步入一个重要的转型时期，个性化教学和英语实用能力的培养成为其显著特征。

《大学英语教学改革基本思路》中指出"掌握英语的目的是为了交流，英语教学应摆脱传统的知识型学习方式。应以技能性学习方式为重点，提高学生的英语应用能力，尤其是口语听说能力，即提高学生用英语在本专业领域的口语和文字交流能力"。

教材是学生学习的中心内容、语言输入的主要来源和教师组织教学活动的主要依据，我们秉承"实用为主，够用为度，学以致用，触类旁通"的原则，为学生编写了《ESP综合英语教程：读写分册1》。

该教材涵盖面广，选材丰富，是一本科学性、实用性、针对性都很强的大学英语教材。教材注重能力与知识并重，有机地将英语基础知识与岗位知识相结合，体现了《大学英语教学改革工程草案》中提出的"避免重复性教学，加强实用英语的训练，将大学英语教学与专业课教学相结合，培养学生的专业英语应用能力。"

总体来说，该教材具有以下特点：

1. 实用性。

教材注重基础词汇的复习和专业词汇的补充，着重培养和训练学生初步具有与其日后职业生涯所必需的英语交际能力。

2. 仿真性。

教材的主体部分为针对具体工作岗位的情景对话，以及在此情景中所能应用的短语和句型，力求帮助学生在仿真语境中进行英语学习。

3. 知识性。

教材涵盖面较广，包括问候介绍、日程安排、招聘和申请、面试、谈判、通知公告和便条、信函、商务旅行以及餐饮等方面的知识。

4. 针对性。

教材针对性较强，注重提高实用英语应用能力。

由于水平有限，错误及疏漏之处在所难免，恳请批评指正。

编　者
2013.9

Contents

Unit 1 Greetings and Introductions 1
    Unit Aims 1
    Warming Up 1
    I. Giving Greetings 2
    II. Making Introductions 3
    III. Greeting and Introduction Languages 6
    IV. Practicing 7
    V. Optional Reading 8

Unit 2 Agenda and Schedule 10
    Unit Aims 10
    Warming Up 10
    I. Arranging Activities 11
    II. Making Meeting Agenda 13
    III. Important Expressions 16
    IV. Practicing 17
    V. Optional Reading 19

Unit 3 Recruitment and Application 21
    Unit Aims 21
    Warming Up 21
    I. Recruitment 22
    II. Application 26
    III. Languages 31
    IV. Practicing 32
    V. Optional Reading 34

Unit 4 Telephoning 37
Unit Aims 37
Warming Up 37
I. Taking Messages 38
II. Making Appointments 40
III. Phoning Languages 41
IV. Practicing 43
V. Optional Reading 44

Unit 5 Interview 47
Unit Aims 47
Warming Up 47
I. Interviewing Process 48
II. Interview Strategies 50
III. Interview Languages 53
IV. Practicing 54
V. Optional Reading 55

Unit 6 Negotiating 58
Unit Aims 58
Warming Up 58
I. Negotiating Procedure 59
II. Discussing Terms and Conditions 61
III. Negotiating Languages 63
IV. Practicing 64
V. Optional Reading 66

Unit 7 Notice and Note 68
Unit Aims 68
Warming Up 68
I. Notice 68
II. Note 75
III. Types of Notes 77
IV. Practicing 80
V. Optional Reading 80

Contents

Unit 8 Business Letters **82**
    Unit Aims 82
    Warming Up 82
    I. Parts of a Business Letter 83
    II. Basic Principles of Writing a Business Letter 85
    III. Basic Phrases and Expressions 86
    IV. Samples of Business Letters 87
    V. Practicing 95
    VI. Optional Reading 97

Unit 9 Business Travel **99**
    Unit Aims 99
    Warming Up 99
    I. Check In 100
    II. Check Out 101
    III. Airline Reservation 102
    IV. Relevant Languages 103
    V. Practicing 105
    VI. Optional Reading 106

Unit 10 Catering **107**
    Unit Aims 107
    Warming Up 107
    I. Table Reservation 108
    II. Receiving the Guest in the Restaurant 109
    III. Taking Orders 111
    IV. Serving Dishes 112
    V. Catering Languages 113
    VI. Optional Reading 114

Unit 1 Greetings and Introductions

Unit Aims

- To learn how to give greetings and respond to greetings
- To learn how to make introductions and respond to introductions
- To master the basic expressions of greetings and introductions
- To learn cultural knowledge about greetings and introductions

Warming Up

Adele Manser is the secretary for the sales department in LRT Software, a multinational company based in Bruchsal Germany. One of her responsibilities is to organize the annual sales meeting and greet the participants when they arrive.

With your partner, make a list of phrases that she can use to greet visitors in English.

Hello, good morning.
Nice to meet you.

1. GIVING GREETINGS

Read the following two dialogues between Adele and two participants who just arrived at the sales meeting.

Dialogue 1:

Adele: Good morning. Are you here for the sales meeting?

John: Yes, my name is John Smith. I'm from the Madrid sales office. I'm the new director of marketing and distribution.

Adele: Nice to meet you, Mr. Smith. I'm Adele Manser, the sales department secretary.

John: Nice to meet you, too, Ms. Manser.

Adele: Mr. Smith, here's your name tag. The conference room is at the end of the corridor over there. Please help yourself to coffee and cookies.

John: Thank you.

Dialogue 2:

Adele: Good morning, Dave, nice to meet you.

Dave: Nice to meet you, too, Adele. How are you?

Adele: Everything is fine, thank you. How about you?

Dave: Not bad. Oh, I'd like you to meet Jane Brown, our department manager. Jane, this is Adele Manser, the sales department secretary of LRT Software.

Adele: Nice to meet you, Ms. Brown. Welcome to the meeting. I hope you enjoy your stay in Bruchasal.

Jane: Thank you, and nice to meet you, too.

1. According to the two dialogues, which visitor does Adele already know?

   Answer: _____

Unit 1 Greetings and Introductions

2. Fill in the blanks in the table below and figure out which greeting and response most probably occurs between old acquaintances and which does not.

Greetings	*Responses*
How do you do?	
	Pleased to meet you, too.
How are you doing?	
How's it going?	
	Couldn't be better, thank you.

3. Complete the dialogue with the given expressions below.

> ★ Long time no see. ★ How's it going?
> ★ I'm great, thanks, how about you? ★ Very well, thank you.
> ★ Pleased to meet you.

A: Hello, Adele. _____. _____?
B: _____, Wilma, _____?
A: _____. Adele, do you still remember Rachel O'Donnell?
B: Sorry, I'm not sure whether we've met before.
A: She is my personal assistant. Rachel, I'd like you to meet Adele Manser, the sales department secretary in LRT.
C: _____.
B: Pleased to meet you, too.

II. MAKING INTRODUCTIONS

Read the following dialogue, and answer the questions:
1) How well does Adele know the two guests, Peter Schmidt and Fritz Armstrong?
2) Has Adele met them before?

Peter: Good morning, you must be Adele Manser. I'm Peter Schmidt from EDS, Bristol, UK.
Adele: Yes, I'm Adele. Good morning, Mr. Schmidt, it's nice to finally meet you face to face.
Peter: Yes, we've talked so much on the phone. I feel like I know you already. Adele, I'd like to introduce to you Fritz Armstrong, our customer services manager. Fritz, this is Adele Manser, the secretary of sales department in LRT.

Fritz:	Nice to meet you, Ms. Manser.
Adele:	It's nice to meet you, too, Mr. Armstrong. How was your flight from Bristol?
Fritz:	It was fine. It even arrived a bit early.
Adele:	That's great. Mr. Armstrong, please follow me this way. Is this your first time in Bruchsal?
Fritz:	No, it's my third. I've been here a couple of times as a tourist. I really like the city.
Adele:	Here we are. This is the conference room. May I take your coat?
Fritz:	Oh, that's very kind of you.
Adele:	Would you care for coffee or tea?
Fritz:	Tea would be nice, with two sugars, please. Thank you very much, Ms. Manser.

1. Now add phrases from the dialogue to fit the categories below.

Introductions	Small talks
_____	_____
_____	_____
_____	
_____	

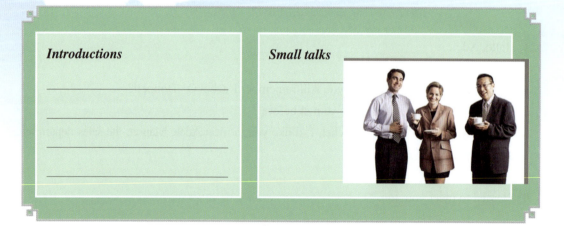

Small Talk

    Small talk may seem to deal with unimportant topics, but it's necessary for "breaking the ice" with customers. People can relax and get comfortable with light topics such as

    ★ Their trip
    ★ Where they're staying
    ★ (First) impression of the city
    ★ The weather

Be careful with making small talk on topics

Unit 1 Greetings and Introductions

like family, religion, politics or with making compliments about somebody's appearance. Depending on your customers' cultural background, they might find the topics too aggressive or too personal in a business context.

2. During the meeting, Adele needs to introduce some of the sales representatives from different countries to other visitors. Work with your partners, and introduce the following sales rep as Adele does.

   E.g. *Please allow me to introduce Peter Schmidt from Bristol. He's British, and he's the sales rep of the EDS Company, Bristol.*

Andrea Bauer	Andy Liu	Marie Chardin	Dennis Filmore
Secretary	Manager	Sales rep	CEO
German	Chinese	Italian	American

Reference Language

Nationalities		Job titles
Austrian	Australian	Accountant
Brazilian	British	Receptionist
French	Irish	Technician
Japanese	Dutch	Personal assistant
Spanish	Swedish	Department manager
Swiss		Sales representative

First Name or Title?

When meeting an English speaker for the first time, address the person with a title and surname (eg. Mr. Smith). For women, the best alternative is Ms (pronounced Mizz) for married and single women. To introduce yourself, use your first name and surname, without a title.

Wait for permission before using first names. In new British industries, the use of first names is more and more usual, but not in traditional companies. Most Americans offer to use first names immediately. This doesn't mean that they want to be close friends; it is simply normal in US business to use first names only. However, be careful—some English speakers, especially managers, still prefer to be called Mr. or Ms.

III. GREETING AND INTRODUCTION LANGUAGES

First time meeting

A: Nice/glad/pleased to meet you.   B: Nice/glad/pleased to meet you too.
A: It's a pleasure to meet you.   B: It's my pleasure to meet you too.
A: I'm excited/ delighted to meet you.   B: Glad to meet you too.
A: How do you do.   B: How do you do.

Between acquaintances

A: Good afternoon/morning!   B: Good afternoon/morning!
A: How are you (doing)?   B: I'm very well, and you?
A: How is everything?   B: Not bad. What about you?
A: How are things? /How is it going?   B: Everything is fine. How about you?

Other expressions:

Long time no see. How's everything?
Haven't seen you for ages. How are you doing?
Good to see you again. How's it going?
What brings you here? How are you doing?
What a pleasant surprise. How are you?
What a small world. How are you doing?

Self-introduction

A: I'd like to introduce myself. My name is Jay.
B: Nice to meet you. I'm Tom.
A: Let me introduce myself. My name is Peter.
B: Pleased to meet you. My name is Jenny.
A: Hi, I'm .../ Hello, my name is ...

Unit 1 Greetings and Introductions

Third party introduction

A: May I introduce you to our manager, Mr. Lee?
B: Yes, please. Pleased to meet you, Mr. Lee.
A: I'd like you to meet Jane Brown, our department/line manager.
B: Nice to meet you, Mr. Brown. My name is Tom Jackson.
A: Let me introduce you to .../ I'd like to introduce you to .../ This is ...

Small talk questions

How was your flight?
Did you have any trouble finding us?
How's your hotel? Everything is OK?
Have you ever been to ...?
What do you think of ...?
Great weather, isn't it? How's the weather in...?

IV. PRACTICING

1. Adele is introducing her company LRT to the visitors. Fill in the blanks in the text about LRT below.

LRT __1__ (be) a leading provider of e-business tools. We __2__ (offer) the solutions and services that companies __3__ (need) to reach their goals. Our customers __4__ (use) our Internet software for a variety of business applications. The LRT e-business platform __5__ (help) companies, their employees, customers, and partners work together successfully. We __6__ (not/sell) software—we __7__ (deliver) solutions __8__ (you/want) to learn more about LRT?

2. Complete the sentences with words from the box below.

| care | contact | finally | get | introduce | journey |
| kind | like | long | may | pleasure | |

1. It's nice to _____ meet you face to face.
2. It was a _____ to meet you. Have a nice _____.
3. May I _____ you to Mrs. Delfino? She's our regional manager.
4. I'd _____ to introduce myself. My name's Alex Brown. I'm the floor manager here.
5. _____ I take your jacket?
6. Oh, that's very _____ of you.
7. Would you _____ for coffee or tea?

8. Can I _____ you some mineral water?
9. We'll be in _____ by emails as usual.
10. So _____ for now.

3. Work within groups of three to practice greetings and introductions. Use the dialogue in Part II to help you or make a dialogue that fits your own situation. You need to introduce yourself, one of your group members and greet properly. Remember asking a couple of "small talk" questions to show your hospitality.

V. OPTIONAL READING

Proper Business Etiquette for Greeting People
By Cindy Anderson

In the business world, if you do not make a good first impression, you may not get another chance. According to an article in *Psychology Today*, people will make judgments about you in as little as 20 seconds, based upon their first impression. So knowing how to greet a person in a confident and friendly manner is extremely important. By using these simple strategies, you will be able to get off to a good start.

Face-to-Face Greeting

Standing up and coming out from behind a desk to greet someone is a good strategy because it gives the impression that you have enough respect for the person to greet them eye-to-eye. Remaining behind a desk puts you in an authoritative position (not equal to the newcomer), which could be perceived as unfriendly or disrespectful.

Friendly, Confident Facial Features

Making an effort to display a genuine smile and looking the newcomer in the eye show that you are friendly and confident. According to *Psychology Today*, others are very good at reading your facial expressions (and making judgments based upon them).

Introduction and Handshake

When you introduce yourself, you should say your first and last name, as in, "Hello, I'm

Unit 1 Greetings and Introductions

Joan Smith." This is more formal than just giving your first name and is appropriate for a first-time greeting. The handshake also gives an important impression of you and must be done properly. Either party may extend their hand first, and you should grip firmly, but without undo strength. (Remember, it is not a contest.) The handshake only needs to last about 3 to 4 seconds.

Elevator Speech

It is very useful to develop what is often called an "elevator speech", or a 20 to 30 second description of your role in the business. It is called so because it is supposed to be brief enough to tell to a fellow elevator passenger on the way down (or up). A practiced elevator speech will help you to become more polished in the introduction of yourself. These are especially useful if you will be attending meetings or receptions where you will have to introduce yourself to the new people.

Unit 2　Agenda and Schedule

Unit Aims

- To master the format and use of an agenda
- To understand the passages and the related information
- To write an English agenda independently

Warming Up

It's said that time is money. When money is used up, it can be back. However, when time is lost, we never get it back again. So we should cherish time, and arrange our time properly. Then we need a schedule. Today we will study how to make schedules and agendas.

1. Do you think it necessary to draw up a schedule before doing something? Why or why not?
2. Have you ever had a plan for study? What are the advantages of making a schedule for your work?
3. Do you have a class timetable? If yes, try to write it down.

Unit 2   Agenda and Schedule

I. ARRANGING ACTIVITIES

1. Read a letter about activity arrangement and an itinerary carefully.

A letter about activity arrangement

Dear Mr. / Ms,

    We are very pleased to welcome President Tom Clinton and Manager Lily Rogers to Jinan and Wuhan in May for about a week. As requested, we propose the following itinerary for your consideration.

Monday, May 8

    2:00 p.m. Arrive in Jinan by Flt.519, to be met at the airport by Mr. President of Shandong Trading Co.

    2:15 p.m. Leave for Quancheng Hotel

    6:30 p.m. Dinner given by President Xie

Tuesday, May 9

    9:00 a.m. Discussion at Shandong Trading Co. Building

    2:00 p.m. Group discussion

    7:30 p.m. Cocktail reception given by the French Commercial Counselor

Wednesday, May 10

    9:10 a.m. Discussion

    11:30 a.m. Sign the Letter of Intent

    12:30 p.m. Dinner

    2:00 p.m. Visit the Baotuquan Park

    7:00 p.m. Departure for Wuhan

Would you please confirm by fax so that we can make arrangements accordingly?

Yours faithfully

Itinerary for Mr. Eckhard Kellermann

July1 to July 5

Note: All times are local times.

Hotel addresses and phone numbers are on attached sheet.

Monday, July 1 (Beijing to New York, the United States)

    9:00 a.m. Leaves Beijing International Airport for Chicago CCAC Flight 982

    12:25 noon Arrives at Chicago International Airport

    12:50 noon Leaves Chicago International Airport for New York

2:10 p.m. Arrives at New York National Airport. Mr. James Keith and Miss Diana Parson meet plane and drive Mr. Eckhard to his hotel, Holiday Inn

6:30 p.m. Dinner at hotel

Dine with Mr. Manfred Hombey (New York office director) and Miss Marianne Taylor (Washington office director)

Tuesday, July 2 (Meeting in New York)

9:00 a.m. Staff meeting at New York Branch Office (Papers in briefcase)

12:00 noon Lunch with office executives

2:00 p.m. Meeting with Mr. Antonio Aurizio, Saturn Corporation at New York Branch Office (Contracts in briefcase)

Wednesday, July 3 (Meetings)

9:10 a.m. Meeting with executives of the Oldsmobile Company at their headquarters

3:30 p.m. Meeting with Robert Clark at their headquarters

Thursday, July 4 (Flights to Beijing)

10:00 a.m. Arrives at National Airport

12:00 a.m. Leaves National Airport for Chicago American Airlines Flight 707

4:00 p.m. Arrives at Chicago International Airport

6:00 p.m. Leaves Chicago for Beijing CAAC Flight 981

Friday, July 5

8:00 a.m. Arrives at Beijing International Airport

Tips

1. The definition of itinerary or activity arrangement

Itinerary or activity arrangement means a plan of journey including places seen and visited. Secretaries should make itineraries for their bosses and coming visitors if they want to go traveling. Itineraries include, apart from the times of arrival and departure of planes and trains, the times and places of specific activities and so on in order to make it convenient for their bosses and coming visitors.

2. How to write schedules

A schedule is a diagram showing tasks and their sequence. It serves to order events. The process of creating a schedule is called scheduling. Scheduling refers to deciding who will do what, and when and where they will do it. When scheduling, we should cover all the necessary information about tasks, length of time per task (or: duration), start and stop times, and sequence of tasks.

Unit 2   Agenda and Schedule

1. Try to find out information in Itinerary for Mr. Eckhard Kellermannto and fill in the blanks.

Schedule			
Day	Time	Place	Task
	____~____		
	____~____		
	____~____		
	____~____		
	____~____		

2. Find the verbs in Box A that go together with the nouns in Box B, then choose three collocations and write sentences. There is often more than one answer.

A	to manage to provide to give to send to read to deliver to speak to produce to join to have to sell to book
B	a company a package a demonstration an email a report a service a language a product lunch a letter a flight dinner a presentation

II. MAKING MEETING AGENDA

Creating an effective agenda is one of the most important elements for a productive meeting. A meeting agenda can provide an outline for the meeting (how long to spend on which topics) and can be used as a checklist to ensure that all information is covered. Besides, it can make participants know what will be discussed if it's distributed before the meeting, and give them an opportunity to come to the meeting prepared for the upcoming discussions or decisions.

A meeting agenda usually includes the following terms:

★ Reference
★ Name of the sponsor
★ Time of the meeting
★ Title of the meeting
★ Place of the meeting
★ People who will attend the meeting
★ Events in time sequence:
  Event 1.
  Event 2.

There are various conferences in any business organization. The secretary must arrange the time and place for the meeting to be held. Now, please read the following Meeting Agendas.

Sample 1

Jiande Board Meeting Agenda
ACCESS TO CAPITAL BOARD MEETING
DEC. 10, 2011

DATE: DEC. 10, 2011
TIME: 9:00 a.m. to 11:00 a.m.
LOCATION: Meeting room 708, Jiande Corporation Building
　　　　　Jiande Street
　　　　　Haidian District, Beijing
　　　　　Telephone: 010-56679920
CHAIRPERSON: Li Ziming, CEO
PRESENTS: All the board members
1. Opening Remarks　9:00 a.m.
　i) Announce subject
　ii) Review and approval of Agenda

Unit 2 Agenda and Schedule

2. The core content of meeting   9:05 a.m.

   i) Discussing the draft of the annual report of Jiande for the year 2012

   ii) Setting the target sales figures for the year 2012

   iii) Setting the development strategy of 2012

   iv) Setting the upgrading of the office computer network in the head office

BREAK   10:35 a.m.

3. Regional Agency Update 10:45 a.m.

4. Other Business   11:30 a.m.

5. Next Board Meeting

   Date: DEC 25, 2011

   Time: 9:30 a.m.

   Place: Meeting room 708, Jiande Corporation Building

   Jiande Street

   Haidian District, Beijing

6. Close   11:40 a.m.

Sample 2

Meeting Agenda of Newtek Corporation

Time: 9:00 a.m. Friday, March 22, 2010

Place: Processing Zone's Tze-Chiang Auditorium, No. 20 Nan-Er Rd, TEPZ, Tantze Hsiang, Taichung County

I. Opening announcement

II. Chairman's address

III. Reporting items

   1. 2009 business report

   2. Supervisor review of 2009 financial statements

   3. Report endorsement and guarantee conditions

   4. Set forth meeting rules for the Company's board of directors

   5. Report on 2009 private placement of common stock and no further private placement installments during the remaining period

IV. Acknowledgment, discussion and voting items

   1. Submission and acknowledgement of the Company's 2006 financial statements

   2. Submission and acknowledgement of the Company's 2006 earnings distribution plan

3. Submission and vote on the proposal to issue new shares by capital increase by cash and global depository receipt.
4. Submission and vote on proposal for private placement of common stock.
5. Submission and vote on proposed revisions to the Company's Articles of Incorporation.
6. Submission and vote on proposed revisions to the Company's Procedures Governing the Acquisition and Disposal of Assets.
7. Submission and election of directors and supervisors.
8. Submission and vote on proposed removal of non-competing clause for directors.

V. Special motions
VI. Meeting adjourned

III. IMPORTANT EXPRESSIONS

Essential words

opening remark 开幕致词
items 条, 项, 款, 事项
roll call 点名, 名单, 登记表
adjournment 休会；延期
keynote address/ speech 主题发言
postpone, adjourn, put off 推迟, 延期
special express 特快车
direct flight 直达航班
catch an early morning flight 赶早班飞机
be due at (time) 预计……到达

call to order 宣布开会
chairperson (会议)主席, 主持人
AOB(=Any Other Business) 其他事项
section/department head 部门主管
place on the agenda 列入议程
closing speech 闭幕词
direct train 直达车
change in (place) 在……转车
be delayed 晚点
departure time 离港时间

Useful Sentences

★ let me see the draft for our meeting.
★ The minutes shouldn't take too long to review.
★ Is there a way to limit the time?
★ We have some new business.
★ As everyone is here, let's get down to business.
★ Good morning, everyone. My purpose here this morning is to present the problem of…
★ Personally, I'd be in favor of that.
★ Those against, raise your hands.
★ Shall we move on to the next item on the agenda?

Unit 2 Agenda and Schedule

★ I'm sorry to cut you off.
★ I declare the meeting adjourned.
★ In that case, I declare the meeting closed.
★ We have arranged for you to meet the university authority tomorrow morning. Does it fit in your schedule?
★ Here is a copy of the itinerary we worked out for you. Will you have a look at it later?
★ There are some minor details I'd like to mention about the itinerary.

IV. PRACTICING

1. Fill in the gaps with the words from the box to obtain the definition of a business meeting agenda.

   | events   attend   title   business   plan   includes |

   A business meeting agenda is a _____ for a business meeting. It _____ elements such as the time, place, and _____ of the meeting, people who _____ the meeting, and the order of the _____ to occur in the meeting.

2. Next week, you and your partner are having a meeting with five important clients from around the world. Unfortunately, your secretary is ill, so you have to make all the arrangements yourself.
   (1) Look at the pictures below and make a "to do" list for the meeting (invent the details yourself).
   (2) Tick three or four things on your list (but not all).
   (3) Now check your arrangements with your partner. Make a dialogue.

3. When a formal meeting is to be held, as the host or organizer the first thing is to make an agenda or a schedule. There are some sentences about them. Read carefully and decide which one is true and which one is false.
   (1) The most important task for the secretary is to choose a suitable meeting room.
   (2) The agenda provides an outline for the meeting.
   (3) The agenda can be used as a checklist to ensure that all information is covered.
   (4) It's easy to create an effective agenda, and it can be done in a few minutes.
   (5) Even a carefully prepared agenda cannot influence very much the outcome of a meeting.

(6) The first step in preparing a meeting agenda is to send an e-mail stating there will be a meeting, the goal of the meeting as well as the administration details such as when and where it will be.

(7) The second step in preparing a meeting agenda is to ask participants requesting an agenda item to contact you no less than ten days before the meeting.

(8) If an inappropriate request is made, suggest that person send an e-mail or memo instead or recommend that this agenda item be discussed in another meeting.

(9) It doesn't matter much if a scheduled one-hour meeting actually lasts much longer.

(10) You should send the agenda to all the meeting participants the day before the meeting with a reminder of the meeting goals, location, time and duration.

4. Read the following sample of the schedule, translate it into English and then present the schedule.

5月12日 星期一	9:00 a.m. 约见汤姆先生 2:30 p.m. 去机场接安南先生,入住长城饭店
6月19日 星期二	8:30 a.m. 带安南先生到公司参观 2:00 p.m. 和安南先生讨论合同 7:30 p.m. 与安南先生共进晚宴
6月20日 星期三	8:00 a.m. 写总结报告 2:00 p.m. 参加商务会议
6月21日 星期四	8:00 a.m. 参观颐和园 3:20 p.m. 公司职员大会
6月22日 星期五	8:00 a.m. 送安南先生去机场 9:10 a.m. 办理登机手续 10:00 a.m. 起飞时间

5. Write a meeting agenda with the following details.

会议:季度经理会议

时间:2010年11月24日星期一上午9点

地点:第一会议室

议程:

会议开幕10分钟

Unit 2　Agenda and Schedule

评估2010年秋季销售进展

季度财政报告35分钟

讨论下列人员谋求助理会计职位的申请：

Mr. Jill Parson,33岁,现任新科技公司助理会计

Mr. Martin Ball,29岁,现任环球太阳能有限公司财务经理助理

Miss Lisa Simpson,28岁,现任本公司的会计助理

下次会议的时间和地点

V. OPTIONAL READING

Qualifications of an Ideal Agent

Because of its highly service-oriented nature, the travel and tourism industry requires those who work in it to have a broader variety of "high-touch" (interpersonal) and high-tech skills than other professions. This means being both efficient and courteous, patient and resourceful.

Desirable Characteristics

In the changing world of Travel and Tourism, a combination of high-touch and high-tech skills is necessary. The list of desirable characteristics is perhaps longer than the list of business and commercial skills needed by the agency itself. Indeed, it is the skills of the agent that make the company.

Before listing such characteristics, attributes and skills, it is important to see what kind of services the employee is expected to provide.

Customers come to the travel agency to get advice on where to go and what to do. They want their travel planes booked and confirmed. Invariably, they want the best price. Often, they will chop and change their itineraries. They want all this done professionally, thoroughly and politely. To be able to deliver that service then becomes your most important function. In order to do that, you will need:

Creativity: Look at the customer, analyze his or her needs, ask proper questions and then make creative suggestions. Don't forget, that person has come to you for something that he or she could not find by herself on the Internet or elsewhere.

A love for the job: Are you enjoying what you are doing? You should be. If not, it's time to look for another job.

Communication and presentation skills: An ability to present information about your products in a persuasive, courteous and pleasant manner.

Service-mindedness: Never forget that what people are buying from you is something they have worked very hard to save up for. Some may be first-time travelers. Others may be veterans. Either way, they expect you to provide that service. The one thing that the Internet cannot provide is the emotional link of eye contact, a pleasant smile and a warm handshake.

Resourcefulness: Clients often ask difficult questions, and are certainly going to shop around. If you don't have the information they want, you need to know where and how to get it.

Patience: Even after doing your best, you may lose the business. No one can win all the time. You must be able to put these losses behind you, and look forward to the next challenge.

A cool head: Handling customer complaints is becoming an art in itself. Cooling down irate clients, talking them through their problem and solving it, is becoming an skill worth its weight in gold. If you have a background or interest in psychology, this could well be a good field to specialize in.

Qualifications

Multi-Cultural Background: Exposure to different cultures in your young days, such as in school or university, could be a major asset.

Language Skills: The importance of these will rise significantly in the next few years. If everyone speaks some English in a global world, your Unique Selling Proposition will lie in your ability to communicate with people of different cultures in their own language.

Good Organization Skills: The complexity of the Travel and Tourism industry requires a human touch to simplify and sort out. Being able to organize well is a major asset in terms of increased productivity and efficient use of time and financial resources.

Professional Integrity and Ethics: True in any profession, but especially in travel which has its fair share of swindles and scandals. Customers are buying a product they have neither seen nor experienced. Are you offering them the best option?

Team Spirit: No company can survive without it. We are all parts of a much bigger machine. If the parts don't do the job they are designed and programmed to do, the machine stops functioning. It's as simple as that.

Good Knowledge of Geography: Where is Cyprus? How long is the Mekong River? Even if you didn't study it in school or university, there is no shortage of tools to help you with geography, from CD-ROM atlases to travel guidebooks, magazines and TV programs. Of course, there is the Internet, too.

Unit 3 Recruitment and Application

Unit Aims

- To know how to write job advertisements
- To know how to write application letters
- To master the basic expressions of greetings and introductions
- To know some cultural background knowledge

Warming Up

Put the following list of recruitment tasks in the order you think they normally occur.

- ☐ a.   Check or write the job description.
- ☐ b.   Make a job offer.
- ☐ c.   Prepare a person specification.
- ☐ d.   Advertising the job.
- ☐ e.   Shortlist applicants form the first interviewers.
- ☐ f.   Conduct second interviews.
- ☐ g.   Carry out screening and interviews.
- ☐ h.   Select the most suitable candidates.
- ☐ i.   After an employee resigns, analyze the job and consider alternatives for hiring a replacement (e.g. internal staff versus the labor market).
- ☐ j.   Send feedback to unsuccessful applicants.

I. RECRUITMENT

The Recruitment Process begins when you need someone new in the organization, either because an existing staff member has left, or because there is new work to be done. It doesn't finish until after the appointment has been made and you have reflected on any changes that you would make in the future recruitments.

The main stages are identified below.

- ★ Recruitment Activities
- ★ Identify vacancy
- ★ Prepare job description and person description
- ★ Advertise
- ★ Manage the response
- ★ Short-listing
- ★ Visits
- ★ References
- ★ Arrange interviews
- ★ Conduct interviews
- ★ Decision making
- ★ Convey the decision
- ★ Appointment action

Read the following job advertisement for CF Travel Service. What do you think would attract applicants to apply for this job?

Call Center Representative at CF Travel Service—The Office, London

Our Image

At CF Travel Service we're renowned for our high standards of customer service and know that first impressions count.

Our call center creates a rapport with our callers, understanding their needs and providing advice and assistance on all their travel requirements. The responsibilities are varied and include promoting CF's ever expanding range of services, whilst maintaining our high levels of customer service.

Unit 3 Recruitment and Application

The Demands

Speaking to around 200 callers each day, you need to be self-motivated whilst maintaining high levels of accuracy in this busy environment. On your shift pattern there will be a variety of start and finish times including some early mornings and late nights. Don't forget shift work means you might have to work at weekends and bank holidays.

The Interview

The interview process consists of a group interview, which will last approximately one hour. You will then take part in a series of exercises. Our experienced recruitment assessors will monitor your performance and look for specific competencies such as customer relationships, service orientation and attention to detail. If you are successful through the group stage, you will be asked to attend an individual interview with three recruitment assessors. You will be notified of the outcome of this final stage by email.

The Rewards

The starting salary is generous and, as a shift worker, you will also receive a shift allowance. There is an increase to the basic salary on successful completion of your three-month probationary period.

On completion of the probationary period, you will be entitled to a generous holiday allowance and a discretionary benefits package which includes a pension, life insurance, CF discount scheme and concessionary travel.

VOCABULARY ASSISTANT	
rapport (融洽)关系；联系 discretionary 无条件的 renowned 有声望的	concessionary 优惠的；让步的 probationary period 试用期 allowance 津贴

1. Word families

Complete the following sentences with words related to the key word "employ" and "recruit". (You might need to add prefixes or suffixes and change the form.) Here's some help with "employ" to get you started.

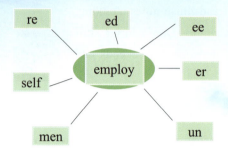

Employ

1. We are unable to use people who are <u>self-employed</u> unless they work for several different companies.
2. There are more people on the job markets when levels of _____ are high.
3. She told her _____ she was looking for another job.
4. We engaged six new _____ in the last quarter.
5. We _____ her in the same position when she returned from maternity leave.

Recruit

6. Last year we _____ two team leaders for our call centre.
7. We've revised our overall _____ procedure because of the new employment legislation.

2. Match these phrases from the CF Travel Service advertisement (1–8) to the definitions (a–h).

(1) to create a rapport
(2) to understand their needs
(3) to provide advice
(4) to promote a range of services
(5) to attend an interview
(6) to be notified of the outcome
(7) to receive a shift allowance
(8) to be entitled to a benefits package

a. to have the right to extra advantages on top of salary
b. to get extra money for working "unsociable" hours
c. to suggest the best way to do something
d. to visit a company to discuss a job
e. to develop a good relationship
f. to be told the results of a decision
g. to attract people's attention to what you offer
h. to know what they want

Unit 3   Recruitment and Application

3. Some applicants had questions about the Job. Supply the answers.

(1) What are the hours of work exactly?
(2) What are the main responsibilities of the job?
(3) How many calls will I have to handle a day?
(4) Where is the job located?
(5) What will the interview consist of and how will we learn the result?
(6) Are there any other payments in addition to the basic salary?
(7) What other benefits do you offer?
(8) Does everyone receive the same benefits package?

Vocabulary for Recruitment	
recruitment 招聘	person specification 个人规范
curriculum vitae 简历	candidate 应试者; 候选人
training 培训	job offer 工作录用通知
selection 甄选	interview 面试
appraisal interview 评估面试	labor market 劳动力市场
job description 职位描述	

Tips for Recruitment

Exchanging information

Can we just have a word about ...
I'd like to be up to date on what's happening.
So where/ what are you planning to ...?
Well, firstly I thought I would ...
I'll look into it (though).

Making suggestions

I suggest we ...   In my opinion ...
What do you think about ...?
Actually, there is someone in the company who ...
Well, we should consider ...

Agreeing and disagreeing

I agree./I disagree.   I think so too.
You have got a point(there).   Yes, that's a good idea.
(I'm)Not sure I agree with you there.

II. APPLICATION

Read the following passage about application letter and CV, and discuss how to write them.

A letter of application

Here is Ingmar koster's letter of application to Bowman International plc for a job as Key Account Manager.

Ingmar D Kosters
27 Church Street
Waterlooville
Hants
P014 5BT

Bowman International plc
HR Dept
Kilburn High Road
London NW6 7JR
27 August 20.

Dear Sir or Madam

    In response to your recent job listing on your website, I am sending you my personal profile as an attachment. I hope you will consider my application for the post of Key Account Manager (Europe).

    With a degree in Business Administration from Cologne University and more than 3 years experience in sales functions (1 year with a Portsmouth—based manufacturing company), I feel I fully meet your requirements. In my current function as account manager, I am responsible for developing existing business contacts abroad. As a native German with considerable exposure to an English-speaking environment, I also have some knowledge of French and Spanish. In the position you advertise on your website I would like to develop my potential as a successful customer relationship manager and establish new business contacts, thus contributing to the continued growth of your company.

    My track record to date is well documented in my personal profile. If there is any further information you may require to shortlist me as one of the possible candidates for the advertised post you can contact me under ingmarkoesters @cellnet.com or 07802 345123.

I would welcome the opportunity of a personal interview and look forward to hearing from you.

Thank you for your time and consideration.

Yours faithfully
Enclosure

A CV

Ingmar D Kosters
27 Church Street
Waterlooville
ants P014 5BT
Tel: 07802 345123
ingmarkoesters@cellnet com

Career objective: Responsible position in sales/customer relationship function with international customer base

Personal data: Born 19 September 19···
German
Single

Qualifications: Abitur (A-level equivalent) with Mathematics and English as main and German and History as subsidiary subjects (average grade: 23) (1993)
Course in Economics at Cologne University 199—2000
Exchange student at Leeds University 1996—1997
Diploma examination in Business Administration with Marketing Finance and Controlling as fields of specialization (final grade: 27) (2000)

Work experience: 2—3 month practicals with
— Schubert GmbH in Cologne 1994 (general office work)
— Mayer & Co KG in Neuss 1995 (distribution)
— Fowler Ltd in Bradford 1997 (logistics & warehousing)
— Baines & Sons Ltd in Leeds 1998 (sales)
— 2000—2002 Sales clerk at Preuss Maschinen GmbH, responsible for customer group based in Germany & Benelux countries
— 2002 to present Account Manager at Marine Engineering Ltd in Portsmouth, responsible for development of French customer base

Military service: 1993—1994 in German Air Force

Other skills: Languages: German (native)

                        English (near native)

                        French (fairly fluent)

                        Spanish (fair)

              PC—literate (common software applications)

              Clean driving license

Interests: Foreign languages and cultures, traveling, ball sports

References available—upon request

Tips

1. Now add phrases from the dialogue to fit the categories below.

A job application is usually made up of several parts:

— the cover (ing) letter or letter of application,

— the CV (curriculum vitae) or resume or personal data sheet (PDS), and

— certificates and testimonials (unusual in Britain or the U.S.A.).

An application can be either solicited (the applicant replies to a job advertisement) or unsolicited (the applicant acts on his/ her own initiative).

The cover letter and the CV are the applicant's most important selling tools. Recruiters often shortlist candidates on the basis of the information provided in these documents. Therefore they should give comprehensive information about the person, the qualifications, experience and skills of the job applicant.

2. How to write a letter of application

The cover letter should not be longer than about 20 lines. It has four parts:

Opening	Solicited application: refer to the job advertisement and say which job you are applying for. Unsolicited application: refer to recently obtained qualification or state reason for intended job change. Say which job you are applying for.
Qualifications and skills	State the qualifications, skills and experience that make you particularly suitable for the job.
Motivation	Write why you are applying and what you hope to achieve in the new post.
Close	State that further information can be given if necessary and when you are available for an interview. Say that you would appreciate a positive reply.

3. How to write a CV

The CV gives a full account of the candidate's education, qualifications and experience. It should be no longer than one page. Note: unlike German CVs, a photo is not included in the UK or in the U.S.A. There are usually five sections in the CV:

1. Personal data	Give your address, telephone number and email address, as well as personal information: age (or date and place of birth). To prevent discrimination, there is very little personal information (i.e. regarding sex, marital status, religion) in British or American CVs.
2. Education	Give details Of your school career and your college or university qualifications State subjects and grade in final exam.
3. Job/work experience	State where and when you trained for a job. Mention work experience including practicals or internships.
4. Skills and activities	State other qualiftcations and skills that may be helpful in your job (1anguages, IT skills, training courses relevant for the job, interests and spare time activities).
5. Reference	British and American CVs usually have the following sentence at the bottom of the page "References supplied (up)on request". This is because employers do not normally write lengthy testimonials about an employee's work and abilities. Instead, they usually give a reference when asked. The applicant will give the address if necessary.

Note: CVs are not signed or dated. They often provide information in reverse chronological order, i.e. starting with the most recent events and then going back.

Useful phrases

Introduction—source of information and application

From your advertisement of ... in the ... I see that you have a vacancy for a(an) ...

Referring to/With reference to your advertisement in today's issue of ... I would like ...

It was with great interest that I read your advertisement in the ... for ... .

From your company website I note that you are inviting applications for the post of ...

I am responding to your recent job listing on your website.

Having graduated from ... with a degree in ..., I am now looking for a traineeship in the ... industry

Information about qualifications

I have considerable experience of this kind of work.

I feel that I can meet the requirements of this post.

I have been working at ... for three years now and gained valuable experience in ...

I have a diploma/qualifications in ...

I was promoted to ...

I am responsible for overseeing approximately eight projects each year.

As important, I need to work well with people—liaising with clients and ...

Motivation and reasons for application/job change

I wish to make use of my knowledge of languages.

I am keen to broaden my knowledge in the field of ...

I am looking to progress from working on local accounts to those of a national and international nature.

Your job offers me the opportunity to do this.

I like responsibility and enjoy the challenge of new situations.

Closing paragraph

I should be pleased/happy to provide you with any further information/any other details you may require.

You will find enclosed/attached a copy of my curriculum vitae which will give you further particulars/more complete details of my qualifications/career to date.

I would greatly appreciate being given the opportunity of an interview.

I hope that you will consider my application favorably.

2.1 List the main points of the letter.

2.2 Find the information in the CV.

1. Describe in which field Ingmar would like to work.
2. Say in which field he specialized during his studies.
3. List the areas in which he obtained some practical experience.
4. Say in which areas he worked with customers.
5. List his language skills.

III. LANGUAGES

Useful Words

personal profile 个人简介
family name, surname *n.* 姓
date of birth 出生日期
born on 出生于
single 单身
widowed 丧偶
education *n.* 教育
primary education 小学教育
junior / primary school（英国7至11岁儿童上学的）小学 /（英国5至11岁儿童就读的）小学
subsidiary subject 辅修课程, 兼修
graduate 大学毕业生
post-graduate 研究生
testimonial, certificate *n.* 证书；证明
B. A (Bachelor of Arts) 文学学士
M. A (Master of Arts) 文学硕士
vocational school 职业学校
vocational qualification 职业证书
in-service training 在职培训
apprenticeship *n.* 学徒期, 实习期
job / work experience 工作经验
occupational *a.* 职业的, 与职业有关的
to work freelance 自由职业
temping *n.* 打零工
probationary period 试用期
paid holiday 带薪休假

CV (curriculum vitae), resume, personal data sheet (PDS) 履历, 个人简历
place of birth 出生地
family status 家庭状况、家属状况
married 已婚
divorced 离异
educational background 教育背景
infant school 幼儿学校
secondary / high[US]school 中学 / 高中（美国）
to attend school / a course 上学, 就读,（学生）上课
main subject, major 主修课程, 专业
mark, grade 分数, 等级
undergraduate 本科生
school leaving certificate 毕业证明
higher / tertiary education 高等教育 / 大学教育
B. Sc. (Bachelor of Science) 理学学士
M. Sc (Master of Science) 理学硕士
vocational training 职业培训
further training 深造
traineeship 实习单位
internship, clerkship, practical *n.* 实习生
professional career 职业生涯
profession *n.* 职业；行业
to work full-time 全职
employment contract 就业合同
pay package 综合工资
working hours 工时

Useful sentences

Introduction—source of information and application

From your advertisement of ... in the ... I see that you have a vacancy for a(an) ...
Referring to / With reference to your advertisement in today's issue of ... I would like ...
It was with great interest that I read your advertisement in the ... for ...

From your company website I note that you are inviting applications for the post of ...

I am responding to your recent job listing on your website.

Having graduated from ... with a degree in ..., I am now looking for a traineeship in the ... Industry.

Information about qualifications

I have considerable experience of this kind of work.

I feel that I can meet the requirements of this post.

I have been working at ... for three years now and gained valuable experience in ...

I have a diploma / qualifications in ...

I was promoted to ...

I am responsible for overseeing approximately eight projects each year.

Motivation and reasons for application/job change

I wish to make use of my knowledge of languages.

I am keen to broaden my knowledge in the field of ...

I am looking to progress from working on local accounts to those of a national and international nature.

Your job offers me the opportunity to do this.

I like responsibility and enjoy the challenge of new situations.

Closing paragraph

I should be pleased / happy to provide you with any further information / any other details you may require.

You will find enclosed / attached a copy of my curriculum vitae which will give you further particulars / more complete details of my qualifications / career to date.

I would greatly appreciate being given the opportunity of an interview.

I hope that you will consider my application favorably.

IV. PRACTICING

1. Match the terms in box A with the appropriate definitions in box B. There are more items than you need.

    A

    (1) ability to enter data into the computer

    (2) able to do basic maths

    (3) able to work with a computer

    (4) current stage of development in technology

    (5) description of the work content

    (6) list of persons working in rotation and their periods of work

    (7) motivation to achieve sth.

Unit 3 Recruitment and Application

(8) non-cash parts of the pay package (company car, business class travel)
(9) person with a university degree
(10) required as a condition for sth.
(11) speaking a language very well
(12) taking the initiative

B

a. computer-literate   b. drive   c. fluent   d. graduate caliber
e. job profile   f. keyboard skills   g. negotiating skills h. numerate
i. prerequisite   j. proactive   k. rota   l. state-of-the-art
m. telephone manners

2. **Link the incomplete sentences 1—8 with the appropriate section a—j to form meaningful sentences. There are two more items than you need**.
   1. It is with great interest that ...
   2. Having just completed my training as foreign language secretary at the Carshalton College ...
   3. As you will see from the enclosed CV ...
   4. During my three month practical at the Logica office in Leatherhead ...
   5. I am confident that with my experience in door-to-door selling.
   6. I attended courses at the Boston Academy for Adult Education.
   7. After graduating from high school I spent two years working in France and Germany.
   8. I hope that you will find my qualifications and skills useful for your business ...

   a. ... and look forward to being invited to an interview
   b. I can make a useful contribution to the Success of your telesales team
   c. I hold a general degree in French and German from Thames University.
   d. I read your advertisement for the post of account manager in today's issue of the Yorkshire Post.
   e. I was able to further develop my secretarial and administrative skills.
   f. I wish to apply for the advertised post of PA to the export manager.
   g. In order to get some practical marketing experience in an English language environment.
   h. ... and as a result I am now fairly fluent in both languages.
   i. ... to further upgrade my computer literacy and keyboarding skills.
   j. ... where I enrolled for a course in business administration.

3. Arrange the sentences of this cover letter in the right order.

Dear Madam, Dear Sir

a. Although the university course was largely literature-oriented, I feel that it has greatly enhanced my analytical and linguistic skills.

b. As part of the course I spent my third year as a Socrates exchange student in Bochum and Orleans where I also attended classes in Business German and Business French.

c. During my four year course at Strathclyde University I read German and French Language and Literature and I graduated with a Joint Honors degree in both these subjects.

d. Enclosed you will find my complete personal profile and also two references.

e. I note with interest from the careers office at Strathclyde University that you are recruiting graduates with an honors degree in foreign languages.

f. I am available to come for an interview at any time and look forward to hearing from you.

g. I am sure that the trainee programme described on your website will provide me with the necessary business background and help me to contribute more effectively to the tasks of an international organization such as yours.

h. I would like you to consider my application for one of these posts.

i. If there is any further information you require do not hesitate to contact me under 01372 584321.

j. In my holidays I gained some practical experience working for companies in my home town so I am familiar with the basic secretarial duties.

k. Yours faithfully.

V. OPTIONAL READING

Looking for a job

Information about job vacancies can be obtained from a variety of sources:

Job advertisements (daily/ weekly papers and some specialist magazines), job exchanges on the internet and company websites, employment/ recruitment agencies (esp. in English speaking countries), government-run offices (in Britain the "Jobcentre"), word of mouth information from personal contacts, career centers in educational establishments or company notice boards

It is quite common for British and American companies to roughly indicate the salary that can be expected (often in the short form of c.20K, i. e. in the range of 20, 000 per annum excluding benefits) Very often a telephone number and the name of a contact person (frequently just the first name) at the end of the advertisement allows candidates to get additional information about the job and to ask for an application form.

Unit 3　Recruitment and Application

Job applications are mostly sent in reply to an advertisement offering a particular job (solicited application). But job seekers do also take the initiative and send an unsolicited application hoping their qualifications will be considered when a vacancy arises.

The application documents include the letter of application and possibly the application form, the CV (curriculum vitae) and relevant documents and testimonials. These make up the candidate's profile which are his/her most important "selling tool" at the first stage of the selection process, i.e. until the selectors have made up a shortlist of candidates they want to interview.

Letter of application/cover letter

Together with the CV, the letter of application (or cover letter) is the candidate's most important "selling tool" and needs to convince the reader of his/her qualifications and suitability for the job advertised. Therefore it must be well presented (layout, font), well structured (paragraphs, logic of thought and language), convincing (genuine interest) in order to arouse interest (content) and lead to action (short listing of candidate).

The text itself must not be too long (15 to 20 lines), ideally arranged in three to four paragraphs covering the following points:

　　　1. source of information and application
　　　2. job-specific qualifications
　　　3. motivation and/or suitability for the job
　　　4. availability for the interview and contact

CV (curriculum vitae)

The CV provides full information about the candidate: personal background, education, qualifications, experience and skills, interests. The information is usually presented in tabular form under the following or similar headings: personal data, education, job training and experience, further qualifications and skills, interests.

In English-speaking countries, the CV is not signed or dated. A photo is usually omitted. For reasons of possible discrimination, Americans are not obliged to reveal age, sex, family status, skin colour or religious belief when applying for a job in their country. Americans arrange the information in reverse chronological order and also usually state their career goal below their personal data (name and address).

As candidates get older and work experience takes up more space, the section on the candidate's education will tend to become shorter. In Anglo-American CVs, references are mentioned either by saying that these can be supplied upon request or by giving the names and addresses of two referees who are prepared to say something about the candidate's character, abilities and qualifications. The "Interests" section provides some indirect information on the applicant's personality (social skills, team orientation etc.) and obviously requires careful consideration as regards the "image" certain activities of the candidate may project.

As in the cover letter the information should be presented with the reader very much in mind. This goes for content (the CV should be comprehensive, but do not state every detail) and length. There are no hard and fast rules as to the layout.

Unit 4 Telephoning

Unit Aims

- To know how to take messages when telephoning
- To know how to make appointments when telephoning
- To master the basic expressions about telephoning
- To know some cultural background knowledge about telephoning

Warming Up

Sara Schumann is an administrative assistant at the German headquarters of Apex Industries. She normally works in another office, but the Purchasing Director's assistant is ill today and Sara is filling in for him. And she is preparing a list of English phrases to help her on the phone. What other telephoning phrases can you add to the list?

Good morning.
This is Sara Schumann speaking.
Who's calling, please?

1. TAKING MESSAGES

Read the following two telephone calls between Sara and a caller from England.

Call 1:

Sara: Good morning. Apex Industries. May I help you?

John: Yes, this is John Richards from Customer Zone Software. I'd like to speak to Eva Lang, please. Could you put me through to her?

Sara: Of course, just a moment, please ... Oh, it seems that her line is engaged. Could you hold a moment? Or would you like to leave a message?

John: I'd prefer to hold for just a minute or two.

Sara: Mr. Richards? Thanks for holding. I'm putting you through to Ms. Lang's office now. If you get cut off for some reason, please get back to me.

John: I'm sorry. Could you speak up a bit? I didn't catch that.

Sara: Sure. I'm connecting you now to Ms. Lang's office. If you don't get through, please ring again. We're having some problems with our phone system.

Call 2:

Sara: Good morning, Apex Industries.

John: This is John Richards again. I'm afraid I got cut off when you tried to put me through.

Sara: I'm terribly sorry about that.

John: I really need to get through to Ms. Lang this afternoon. Could I leave a message for her to ring me back as soon as possible?

Sara: Yes, certainly, Mr. Richards. Could I have your phone number, please?

John: Yes, I'm calling from my mobile. It's 0044 7721 332558.

Sara: Right, so, that's 0044 7721 332558. I'll make sure she calls you back today. Could I help you with anything else?

John: Would it be possible to have her mobile number? Could you perhaps look it up for me?

Unit 4　Telephoning

Sara:　　Yes, that's no problem. I've got it right here. It's 49 for Germany, then 1568877944.
John:　　Let me just repeat that. That's 49 1568877944
Sara:　　That's right.
John:　　Ok. Thanks once again. Bye for now.
Sara:　　You're welcome. Goodbye.

1. Now write the message that Sara takes.

 Message

Message for:
Caller:
Company:
Message:

2. Put the following phrases in the categories below.

- One moment please, I'll put you through.
- I'd like to speak to Ms. Lang, please.
- You're welcome. Good bye.
- Thanks for your help.
- Who's calling please?
- What is this concerning?
- Can I take a message?
- Would you like to leave a message?
- Could I speak to Ms. Lang, please?
- Could you please ask her to call me back?
- I'm phoning about the Boston Electronics contract.
- Hello, John Richard speaking.

"This is Apex Industries."

	Take a call	Make a call
Identifying the caller		
Getting through		
Reason for calling		
Taking a message		
Ending the call		

II. MAKING APPOINTMENTS

Read the following dialogue and talk about why the caller needs to change the appointment?

Sara: I'm afraid she's not in her office at the moment. Can I help you?

John: Yes, I hope you can. I have an appointment with Ms. Lang on Thursday, and I'm afraid I can't make it. I'm flying to Chicago on Wednesday evening, so we'll have to postpone our meeting until next week.

Sara: I see. And which day would be convenient for you?

John: How about Tuesday?

Sara: I'm sorry but Ms. Lang is attending a conference on Tuesday. Would Wednesday suit you?

John: That would be fine. At 3:00?

Sara: Yes, that fits her schedule. I'll book you in from 3:00 to 4:00 on Wednesday.

Unit 4　Telephoning

Useful Expressions about Making Appointments

How about Wednesday?

Would Friday suit you?

That would be possible/ convenient.

Yes, that fits her schedule.

I'm sorry, but he's tied up then.

Unfortunately, I have to cancel your appointment.

I'm afraid she's busy on Tuesday.

I'm afraid Ms. Lang can't make it to the meeting on Friday.

III. PHONING LANGUAGES

Phoning somebody

This is John Richard speaking. Can/Could/May I speak to Ms. Lang, please?

Hello, my name is ..., I'm calling to ...

This is John Richard from England.

Answering the phone

Good morning, Apex Industries.

Hello, Sara speaking. How can I help you?

Who's calling/ May I have your name, please?

Putting through

Can/ Could you hold the line, please?

Could you put me through to Ms. Lang, please?

— Of course, one moment please?

Thanks for holding/waiting. I am putting you through to Ms. Lang's office now.

Saying somebody is not available

I'm sorry, but ... is not available/ free at the moment.

I'm sorry, but ... is away/ out of his office today.

I'm sorry, but ... is in a meeting at the moment.

I'm sorry, but ... is speaking on another line at present.

Messages

Could/ Can I take a message for you?

Would you like to leave a message?

Could I leave her a message to ring me back as soon as possible?

— I'll make sure she gets your message straight away.

— I'll make sure she calls you back today.

Asking for information

What was the name again, please?

Can/ could you give me your fax/phone/mobile number, please?

Saying Phone Numbers

★ Say the individual numbers one after the other. Say the number 0 as the letter o (common in British English) or zero (common in American and International English).

★ Never use tens, e.g. "fifty-seven" for "five-seven"
156043   one-five-sixe-oh/zero-four-three

★ Say double and triple numbers like this:
856699   eight-five-double six-double nine or eight-five-six six-nine nine
655589   six-double five five-eight-nine or six-five double five-eight-nine or six-five five five-eight-nine

Can / May I have your email address, please?

Saying Email Addresses

★ Say words in email addresses as complete words but individual letters on their own.
  e.g. dkflower@yahoo.com   d-k-flower

★ say symbols like this:
  @   at
  .   dot
  -    dash
  _   underscore
  /   slash
  \   back slash

Unit 4 Telephoning

> ★ British firms' addresses normally end with .co.uk, said as 'dot co dot uk' ('co' rhymes 'no'). American firms' addresses normally end with .com, said as 'dot com'.
>
> e.g. d_flower@tom.com   d underscore flower at tom dot com
>
> John-Richard@ dsg.co.uk   John dash Richard at d s g dot co dot uk

Finishing the call

Could I help/ assist you with anything else today?

Is there anything else I can help you with today?

I appreciate you taking time to talk to me.

Many thanks for calling us.

IV. PRACTICING

1. Match the statements or questions (1–8) to the responses (a–h).

1. Thank you.	a. Thank you. I really appreciate it.
2. I'm afraid he's not in.	b. Yes, certainly. I'll just get a pen.
3. May I help you?	c. You're welcome.
4. I'll make sure he gets the message straight away.	d. Yes, I have a question about your price list.
5. I'm afraid I got cut off.	e. That's OK. I'll call back later.
6. Could I leave him a message?	f. Yes. It's P-F-A-double F
7. My name is John Richard.	g. Oh, I'm terribly sorry about that. Let me put you through again.
8. I'm sorry. Could you spell that, please?	h. I'm sorry. I didn't quite catch that.

2. Put the following phone conversation in the correct order.

Emma Jones

a. Mia, this is Emma Jones from Band Sports. We met at the trade fair last week.

b. Would Tuesday be convenient for you, at 9 am?

c. Bye.

d. Hello. May I speak to Mia Mitchell, please?

e. Sounds good. Ok, Mia, that's Tuesday at 11 o'clock. I look forward to seeing you.

f. Fine, thanks. Mia, I'm calling to see if we could set up a meeting. You wanted me to do a presentation on our services and I'll be in New York next week.

Mia Mitchell

g. Same here. Thank for calling. Bye.

h. Hello.

i. Next week? Let me just check my diary. What day exactly?

j. Tuesday looks good, but I'm busy at 9. How about 11 o'clock instead?

k. Speaking.

l. Ah, yes. Right. How are you?

The correct order:

3. Read the following sentences to your partner, who should note down the phone numbers, then swap roles.

   1. My number's 0044 for the UK, then 141 for Glasgow, then 6788430.
   2. You can reach me on my mobile. The number's 0164, then 645783.
   3. The number of my hotel is 0566 for Cologne, then 842092.
   4. We've moved. Our new number is 0865 for Constance, then 17965.
   5. Can you fax confirmation, please? The number's 0034 for the Netherlands, then 167 for Gouda, then 990076.
   6. You can phone Rolf direct on 060 for Berlin, then 8796669.

V. OPTIONAL READING

Basic Phone Skills Training

Many businessmen understand that improving the company's image, reinforcing the brand and enhancing customer service are the necessary elements to ultimately boost profits. That's why companies today invest money and time to train employees in telephone etiquette that makes the *most favorable impression.*

Types

Most phone skills training is customized to a company's needs. One type — essential telephone etiquette — would benefit all employees even if they don't interact with customers. Other types boost the goals of specific departments. For example, sales professionals are trained in service-oriented telephone skills, while customer service associates who respond to complaints benefit from problem-solving telephone skills. There are also individual coaching sessions for all staff members or for senior managers, new hire and ongoing employees. Advanced training for sales executives is also available.

Significance

When your customers get to phone conference with employees who address them properly, take time to understand their needs and concerns and look for the most efficient ways to solve their problems, they understand that your company values their business. "Your telephone customer service experience is critical," says the Phone Coach Team, which has helped business people improve their phone skills for 15 years. "If your team members aren't able to connect with customers effectively the telephone experience they create may literally drive customers away."

Benefits

Proper telephone etiquette offers benefits that few businesses take lightly. Chief among the benefits is that employees with good phone skills drive profits for any business, whether it manufactures a product or provides a service. And many companies also understand that answering the phone properly strengthens their brand image. According to business writer Anne M. Obarski, customers will connect your service or product with the telephone experience your employees offer. Obarski's article, "Hello, Your Paycheck Is Calling, Your Phone Skills Can Market Your Unique Brand" quotes business author Dr. Janelle Barlow who said that "reinforcing a brand through every customer touch point, therefore, can provide the repetition necessary to inspire purchasing decisions."

Customization

Phone skills training today is customized to your company's specialty and to each staff member's role. For example, there is relationship selling for call center sales employees. Coach the phone skills and train mentors, supervisors and team leaders, so they can provide ongoing support to employees long after the telephone trainers are gone.

Staff who interact with finicky customers will benefit from the stress buster of phone skills training. There is also a training course for personality styles, which teaches employees how to customize their service so they can satisfy customers who want just the facts, as well as customers who expect more interaction.

Expert Insight

Business experts trying to account for a decline in profits are likely to look at a company's customer service practices. According to the phone skills experts at The Phone Coach, "all problems walk on two feet." When the wrong people are answering the phones, they are creating negative images of your company and pushing your customers far away.

Unit 5 Interview

Unit Aims

- To gain basic knowledge about interview process
- To gain basic knowledge about interview strategies
- To master useful expressions about interview
- To know some more strategies about interviewing and hiring people

Warming Up

Work in groups.

It is never an easy job to interview effectively—even when you have gone on more interviews than you can count. Laura Donaldson, a fresh graduate from the university, is going to participate in an interview. What advice will you give her? See if your tips are listed below. If not, add them to the list.

A. Be punctual for the interview.

B. Applicants should never wear jeans to an interview.

C. Try to relax and stay as calm as possible during the interview.

D. _____

E. _____

I. INTERVIEWING PROCESS

Read the following dialogue between Laura Donaldson and Angela Duncan. Try your best to gain basic knowledge about interview process.

Laura: Excuse me. May I see Mrs. Duncan?
Angela: It's me. What can I do for you?
Laura: Nice to meet you, Mrs. Duncan. My name is Laura Donaldson. I have come for an interview as requested.
Angela: Nice to meet you, too. Thank you for coming. Please take a seat.
Laura: Thank you.
Angela: Could you please tell me a little about yourself? What kind of person do you think you are?
Laura: Generally speaking, I am energetic and diligent. That's my strongest personality.
Angela: Well, from your application form you said you've just left university, I think.
Laura: Yes. I've just graduated from Peking University this July. And I have majored in marketing.
Angela: How did you get on with your studies in university?
Laura: I did well in university. I won the university scholarship for four years on end.
Angela: And what makes you apply for this position as a saleswoman?
Laura: Um... I love meeting people. Being a saleswoman would be a marvelous opportunity to meet people from all walks of life. I have always wanted to travel. It would also be a good chance to put what I have learned to good use. Then there's the challenge of working on my own initiative...
Angela: I see. Well, I don't think there's anything else. Do you have any questions?
Laura: Yes. Could you tell me something about the training program for new employees?
Angela: Yes. It lasts for 6 weeks and aims to give an overall picture of the company, including everything you'll ever need to know about our products, and a thorough grounding in persuasion tactics, mostly through role-play situations. Anything else?
Laura: No, I don't think so.
Angela: Fine, we'll be getting in touch with you in the next couple of days.
Laura: Thank you very much.

Unit 5 Interview

Note down the key information about the candidate.

Name:
Personality:
Major:
University:
The position applied for:
Reasons for application:

Put the following phrases in the categories below, according to the general process of a job interview.

1. And what makes you apply for this position as a saleswoman?

2. How did you get on with your studies in university?

3. Could you please tell me a little about yourself?

4. Could you tell me something about the training program for new employees?

5. Fine, we'll be getting in touch with you in the next couple of days.

6. Thank you for coming. Please take a seat.

7. I've just graduated from Peking University this July.

8. I have come for an interview as requested.

9. What can I do for you?

10. Excuse me. May I see Mrs. Duncan?

11. Thank you very much.

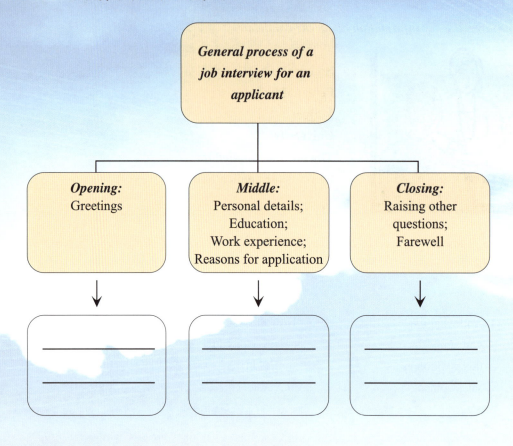

II. INTERVIEW STRATEGIES

Read the following extracts from Angela's interview with Daniel Foster. Pay much attention to what kind of questions Angela asks and what kind of answers she requires.

Angela: I think that fills you in on the requirements of the job. So, could you tell me about your experience as a team leader in your present job?

Daniel: Yes, I've been with my present company for five years. I started as a member of the call centre and was promoted to a team leader two years ago. I'm one of eight team leaders and we cover two shifts, seven days a week.

Angela: Could you explain what that involves?

Daniel: Yes, I'm responsible for ten call centre operators and I report to the call centre supervisor. As you can see from my CV, I also did customer service in a production company for six years before that.

Unit 5 Interview

***

Angela: Could you outline some of the problems you've had to deal with since you became a team leader?

Daniel: Well, they relate mainly to difficult customers and to one or two negative relationships in the group.

Angela: Could you enlarge on that?

Daniel: As far as staff relationships are concerned, if the problem is not solved by discussion and liaison within the team, then we can usually move people to another team. The team leaders meet weekly to discuss the overall situation and we operate a very flexible call centre where the staff can move around different sections to gain more experience.

Angela: And how do you go about dealing with difficult customers or with customers who have a complaint?

Daniel: We have a directive that says that a customer who is not happy about something should be transferred to a team leader immediately. It's one of our specific responsibilities. Otherwise my staff are instructed to tell the customer that I will call them back as soon as possible. If I'm not there, then another team leader deals with it.

***

Angela: What aspect of your job do you like best, Daniel?

Daniel: I particularly enjoy dealing with customers. I think I have an ability to build a good rapport with people on the telephone—this is why I went into this type of work — and I believe I am good at it.

***

Angela: Why do you want to leave your present job?

Daniel: Part of the call centre is being transferred to another location in the South. My wife has a good job in this area and we have two children at school. I don't really want to move at this time, although my company did ask me if I would like to relocate.

Angela: I see. Thank you. As you know, the next part of the interview process would be an assessment centre...

1. **What do these words and expressions from the dialogue mean? Tick the correct definition.**

   1) **to fill someone in** _____ **a.** to complete a form

   _____ **b.** to give more information so they have all the details

   2) **to be promoted** _____ **a.** to move to a higher position in a company

   _____ **b.** to take a lower position in a company

3) **to outline something** _____ a. to summarize
_____ b. to give a detailed explanation

4) **liaison within the team** _____ a. exchange of information between team members
_____ b. a romantic relationship

5) **to complain** _____ a. to say everything is fine
_____ b. to say that you are unhappy about something

6) **directive** _____ a. a rule
_____ b. a special person who deals with something

7) **to relocate** _____ a. to move to a new area (with your job)
_____ b. to be asked to leave your job

2. Read strategies for interviewing questioning as follows. Change these "closed" questions, which could be answered with "yes" or "no", to open ones.

1) Do you get on well with your present supervisor?
2) Have you had many staff problems to deal with in your current job?
3) Do you consider yourself good at customer service?
4) Are you used to working shifts?
5) Are you able to work on your own initiative?
6) Do you work well under pressure?

Strategies for Interviewing Questioning

Look at the type of the interview questions in the dialogue. These are known as "open questions" and usually avoid "yes" and "no" answers. Below are some examples of the way you can word your interview questions to get people to talk about themselves and their experience.

What...?
What aspects of your job do you like best? What do you know about?
What experience have you had of...?

Why...?
Why do you want to leave your present job?
Why did you deal with the situation in that way?

How...?
How do you go about dealing with...?
How would you handle...?

OR
I'd like you to tell me...
Could you give me an example of...?
Interesting. What else do you...?

III. INTERVIEW LANGUAGES

Opening

Excuse me. May I see Mrs. Duncan?
Nice to meet you, Mrs. Duncan.
My name is Laura Donaldson.
I have come for an interview as requested/invited.
I have come at your invitation for an interview.
Nice to meet you, too. Thank you for coming. Please take a seat.

Middle
Personal details

Could you please tell me a little about yourself?
What kind of person do you think you are?
Generally speaking, I am energetic and diligent.
I think I am quite outgoing/easy going.
I'm afraid I'm not very creative.

Education

I've just graduated from Peking University this July.
And I have majored in marketing.
How did you get on with your studies in university?
I did well in university.
I won the university scholarship for four years on end.

Working experience

So, could you tell me about your experience as a team leader in your present job?
Could you outline some of the problems you've had to deal with since you became a team leader?
What aspects of your job do you like best, Daniel?

Qualifications and skills

I have passed CET-6.
I have got a master degree.
I have got a driver's license.
My English is expressive and I can read French.

Closing
Raising questions

Could you tell me something about the training program for new employees?
Do you have a training program for new employees?
I'd like to know if there would be a training program for new employees.

Farewell

Thanks for your time.
Fine, we'll be getting in touch with you in the next couple of days.
You can reach me any time at your convenience.

IV. PRACTICING

1. Order the following interview strategies according to a logical process.

_____ a. Establish rapport and relax the candidate.
_____ b. Read the candidate's application and have it with you at the interview.
_____ c. Use open questions as much as possible to ensure the candidate gives detailed answers.
_____ d. Allow the candidate to do most of the talking but keep the interview focused.
_____ e. Before finishing the interview, explain what will happen next and by when.
_____ f. Use a quiet office away from noise and interruptions.
_____ g. Welcome the applicant warmly, introduce yourself and explain the structure of the interview.
_____ h. Allow the candidate time for his or her own questions.

The correct order:
_____

2. Use the following form to make notes about the interview in Dialogue 2.

Interview notes

Name of applicant: (1) _____
Job applied for: (2) _____

Experience
a. 5 years' experience in a similar position
b. (3) _____
c. (4) _____

Level of responsibility
a. reports directly to call centre supervisor
b. (5) _____
c. (6) _____

Specific abilities
Staff relationships: (7) _____
_____

Unit 5　Interview

Customer service: good communication skills, (8) _____

Reasons for leaving (9) _____

3. **Word families: Complete the following sentences with words related to the key words. (You might need to add prefixes or suffixes and change the form)**

   `apply`
   1) There were two _____ who were far better than the others in terms of previous experience.
   2) All candidates must complete an _____ form to bring to the interview.
   3) The employment legislation is not _____ to people working less than 25 hours per week.

   `select`
   1) As we had a lot of candidates for the advertised position, we were able to be very _____.
   2) We offer a _____ of benefits to our personnel in addition to salary.

   `assess`
   1) In some types of recruitment, _____ centres are used regularly.
   2) It was difficult to _____ the final two shortlisted applicants as they had such mixed skills.

V. OPTIONAL READING

How to Interview and Hire People

Step 1 Prepare. Prior to the interview make sure you understand the key elements of the job. Develop a simple outline that covers the job duties. Possibly work with the incumbent or people familiar with the various responsibilities to understand what the job is about. Screen the resumes and applications to gain information for the interview. Standardize and prepare the questions you will ask each applicant.

Step 2 Purpose. Skilled and talented people have more choices and job opportunities to choose from. The interviewer forms the applicants' first impression of the company. Not only are you trying to determine the best applicant, but you also have to convince the applicants this is the best place for them to work.

Step 3 Performance. Identify the knowledge, attributes, and skills the applicant needs for success. If the job requires special education or licensing, be sure to include it on your list. Identify the top seven attributes or competencies the job requires and structure the interview accordingly. Some of these attributes might include:

- What authority the person has to discipline, hire, and/or fire others and establish performance objectives;
- What financial responsibility, authority, and control the person has;
- What decision-making authority the person has;
- How this person is held accountable for performance objectives for his/her team, business unit, or organization;
- The consequences they are responsible for when mistakes are made.

Step 4 People Skills. The hardest to determine, as well as the most important part of the process, is identifying the people skills a person brings to the job. Each applicant wears a "mask." A good interviewing and selecting process discovers who is behind that mask and determines if a match exists between the individual and the job. By understanding the applicant's personality style, values, and motivations, you are guaranteed to improve your hiring and selecting process.

Obviously many jobs, particularly sales jobs, require a high degree of people contact. By placing someone in this job who dislikes interaction with others would be a mismatch, affecting his or her job performance.

Pre-employment profiles are an important aspect of the hiring process for a growing number of employers. By using behavioral assessments and personality profiles organizations can quickly know how the person will interact with their coworkers, customers, and direct reports. They provide an accurate analysis of an applicant's behaviors and attitudes, otherwise left to subjective judgment. The D.I.S.C. Assessment and the Personal Interests, Attitudes and Values are popular and useful tools.

Step 5 Process. The best interview follows a structured process. This doesn't mean the entire process is inflexible without spontaneity. What it means is, each applicant is asked the same questions and is scored with a consistent rating process. A structured approach helps avoid bias and gives all applicants a fair chance. The best way to accomplish this is by using behavioral based questions and situational questions.

Behavioral Based Questions

Behavioral based questions help to evaluate the applicant's past behavior, judgment, and initiative. Here are some examples:

- Give me an example when you ...
- Describe a crisis your organization faced and how you managed it.
- Tell me about the time you reached out for additional responsibility.
- Tell me about the largest project you worked on.
- Tell me about the last time you broke the rules.

Unit 5 Interview

Situational Based Questions

Situational based questions evaluate the applicant's judgment, ability, and knowledge. The interviewer first gives the applicant a hypothetical situation such as:

"You are a manager, and one of your employees has just told you he thinks another worker is stealing merchandise from the store."

- What should you do?
- What additional information should you obtain?
- How many options do you have?
- Should you call the police?

Unit 6 Negotiating

Unit Aims

- To gain basic knowledge about negotiating procedure
- To learn how to discuss terms and conditions in negotiating
- To master the basic expressions about negotiating
- To know some knowledge about striking a negotiable opening shot

Warming Up

What makes a successful negotiation? Look at the tips below. First work with a partner to rank those tips from most important (1) to least important (10), then add some more tips to the list.

(1) Always listen carefully to the other person.

(2) Be flexible and prepared to compromise.

(3) Be positive—highlight the "common ground".

(4) Build rapport and be courteous.

(5) Use simple and clear language.

(6) Use persuasion, not threats.

(7) Prepare your arguments.

(8) Be constructive and avoid open conflict.

(9) Always remember your aims.

(10) When agreement is reached, summarize clearly and close the deal.

…

Unit 6 Negotiating

I. NEGOTIATING PROCEDURE

Dialogue:

A Wage Negotiation

Allen Macadam, the industrial relations manager, and Edmund Brook, the personnel manager, are now meeting the union representatives, among them Leo Sharp and Eric Cotton, to try to reach an agreement on the pay deal.

Allen: Thank you for calling the meeting. We are happy to meet you today to work out a solution. We'd like to start by welcoming everyone and restating our proposals. Then perhaps you could outline why the offer was rejected by your members. Edmund?

Edmund: Yes. A 3% increase has been agreed, which we consider is a reasonable and fair offer given the current economic situation and the fact that our sales are down. The outlook isn't a very bright one at present, but we think things will improve in the next six to nine months provided we can contain costs. I'd also like to remind you that you had a 3% review a year ago while the salaries of the white-collar workers were frozen.

Leo: But our members aren't happy with 3% and, since overtime was stopped six months ago, they feel they have suffered enough. It's a difficult situation, that's true, but they want a minimum of 5%. What's more, they are threatening industrial action if they don't get it.

Allen: That's a bit unfair, isn't it? I heard there are some rumors going around about transferring work to a French subsidiary. Has this got anything to do with it?

Eric: Yes, that's right. They are worried that the plant is facing closure. That would be a disaster for an area like this which is already facing high unemployment. You know what rumors are like.

Edmund: We'd like to reassure you that, as far as we are aware, there is no plan to close the plant or transfer business to France. Management has asked us to give you their assurances on this point. We've studied the figures and the bottom line is that there's not much money in the pot, so we have to reach a compromise.

Eric: I'm sorry, but why should we believe this? Outsourcing is happening everywhere at present—cheaper labor, cheaper factories...

Allen: Let's not get too hot under the collar, Eric. We consider ourselves to be a fair and responsible employer with a consistent record of commitment and honesty with our employees. Listen, we'd like to put our cards on the table. If your members accept 3% now, we will give a further 1.5% in nine months, as long as there isn't substantial drop in sales. But we want your assurances that there will be no industrial action.

Leo: Could we have ten minutes to talk about it outside?

Allen: Certainly. Let's break for coffee and meet back in 20 minutes.

***

Leo: Ok. We think this is a reasonable compromise. Our members will agree 3% now and 1.5% in nine months. And you have our assurances there will be no industrial action.

Edmund: That's it then. A successful conclusion for everybody. Thank you.

Allen: Good, I'll send you written confirmation tomorrow, which you can post on the notice boards around the shop floor if you like. The 3% review will take effect from 1 March.

1. Discuss the following questions with your partners.

1) What is the main objective of the union representatives?
2) What is the bargaining power of the union representatives compared to their opponent's? And what about Allen and Edmund's?
3) What is the result of this negotiation?

2. Match the following sentences to the five parts of a negotiation.

1) Let's not get too hot under the collar.
2) We'd like to start by welcoming everyone and restating our proposal.
3) But we want your assurances that there will be no industrial action.
4) We are happy to meet you today to work out a solution.
5) That's it, then a successful conclusion for everybody.
6) We have studied the figures and the bottom line is that there's not much money in the pot, so we have to reach a compromise.
7) Management has asked us to give you their assurances on this point.
8) Ok. We think this is a reasonable compromise.

Building rapport: _____
Establishing objectives and aims: _____
Bargaining: _____
Addressing conflict: _____
Concluding: _____

II. DISCUSSING TERMS AND CONDITIONS

Conditional sentences are often used in sales negotiations to discuss terms and conditions. The type of conditional sentences you use depends largely on the message you want to give.

To discuss 'facts' and things which are always true, such as your standard terms and conditions:

When you **order** more than 100 articles, you **get** a 5% discount.

To discuss terms and conditions which you consider very possible:

If you **buy** more than 200 articles, we**'ll give** you a 7% discount.

If we **buy** five more cars, we **will** also **need** a reduction in the overhead costs.

A salesperson might use this form to make the offer more attractive to the buyer, or the buyer might use it to stress a condition they feel strongly about.

To discuss terms and conditions which are less likely, or to show that you are just looking into possibilities:

If you **took** just five more cars, we **could lower** our offer by 5%.

If we **extended** the contract, **would** you **provide** us with a 5% discount?

This form is often used to see how far the other party is willing to go in a negotiation, without making any promises yourself. It is less direct and thus comes across as more polite.

Read the following dialogues concerning sales negotiation.

Dialogue 1:

A: The product is exactly what you're looking for, isn't it?

B: Yes, we're happy with the product, but the price you offered is a little high at the moment. Is there any way you could reduce the price, say with a discount?

A: Well, **if** you **bought** another 10,000, we **would reconsider** our offer.

Dialogue 2:

A: We could think about the delivery dates, perhaps?

B: What do you mean?

A: Well, maybe we **can agree** to order the items in the next few weeks **if** you think you **can come down** a bit on the price.

B: We **will** certainly **reduce** our price **if** you **buy** before the end of the month.

Dialogue 3:

A: We obviously want to create long-term relationships with our customers.

B: Yes, but I'm sure you agree that we also need some benefits for the relationship to continue. **Can** you **guarantee** us cheaper prices **if** we **continue to order** from you?

A: Certainly. Our clients always **get** discounts **when** they **stay** with us overtime.

Dialogue 4:

A: We've really gone down to the lowest possible price now, I am afraid.

B: But it's still not as good as the offer in terms of the service provided. And we've already discussed the fact that the repair costs, for example, will really be very minimal.

A: That is correct. Of course we're convinced of the quality as well, so **I'll include** repair costs in our offer **if** you accept the price as it is.

Dialogue 5:

A: We've been mostly happy with the product so far but, of course, we are always looking at our options. So, in this case, in order to continue ordering from you, we would need these small changes to the contract.

B: But we're not sure that this will still be profitable for us if we agree to these changes.

A: I'm sorry, but we really have no choice. We **could** only **extend** the contract **if** you **agreed** to all the terms.

1. **Work with a partner and decide which (a, b, or c) speakers are talking about.**
   a. Conditions which are facts or always true: _____
   b. Terms and conditions that are very possible for both partners: _____
   c. Possibilities which both partners are considering: _____

2. **Complete the following conditional sentences with the correct form of the verbs in brackets. Use the hints to help you choose the correct form.**

   (1) If we _____ (lease) our entire fleet from them,
   we _____ (receive) a big reduction in the overall costs.   *Looking at possibilities*

   (2) If you _____ (increase) the order by just 50,
   we _____ (can lower) our offer by 5%.   *Making the offer more attractive*

   (3) If we _____ (agree) to your payment schedule,
   we _____ (need) a reduction in the overall costs.   *Stressing an important condition*

(4) If you _____ (agree) to all the other conditions, then I'm sure we _____ (be able to) meet your demands for the delivery time.

Looking at possibilities

(5) When you _____ (buy) our inspection services for a monthly fee, you _____ (receive) a discount for the maintenance fees.

Facts, always true

(6) If it _____ (be) all right with you, I _____ (send) you the draft version of the contract by Wednesday.

Very possible

III. NEGOTIATING LANGUAGES

Starting the conversation

We are happy to meet you today to work out a solution.

We'd like to start by welcoming everyone and restating our proposals.

We're very happy to be meeting you today.

We hope to come to an acceptable solution for both of us.

I'd like to discuss some of the details in the offer.

Persuading

Management has asked us to give you their assurances on this point.

We can reassure you on that point totally.

It would be your advantage to...

It might be in your interest to...

It's the best offer around. You won't find a better one.

Bargaining

If your members accept 3% now, we will give a further 1.5% in nine months, as long as there isn't substantial drop in sales.

If you buy more than 200 articles, we'll give you a 7% discount.

We would agree on one condition.

I'd go along with that on condition that you return to work.

That seems a good compromise, as long as there is no industrial action of any kind.

If you agree to..., we can...

Showing agreement on a point or offer

I agree with you on that point.

That's a fair suggestion.

I think we can both agree that...

I don't see any problem with/ in that.

Showing objection on a point or offer

I'm prepared to compromise, but...

The way I look at it...

The way I see things...

If you look at it from my point of view, ...

I'm afraid I had something different in mind.

That's not exactly how I look at it.

From my perspective, ...

I'm afraid that doesn't work for me.

Is that your best offer?

Concluding your arguments

That's it, then a successful conclusion for everybody.

Ok. We think this is a reasonable compromise.

So that wraps it up.

That sums our side then.

We're sure that you will see the benefits for your company if you take up our offer.

There you have our proposal. I'm afraid that's as far as we can go.

Finishing the conversation

Good, I'll send you written confirmation tomorrow, which you can post on the notice boards around the shop floor if you like.

That may be a possibility but I have to discuss it with my boss.

Let me get back to you.

I'm happy we've found a solution. I'll send you an email tomorrow summarizing our agreement.

IV. PRACTICING

1. Match the words from this unit with the right definitions on the right.

    Outsource   a. an agreement in an argument in which the people involved reduce their demands or change their opinion in order to agree

Unit 6 Negotiating

Overtime	**b.** something which you plan to do or achieve
Compromise	**c.** a formal suggestion, plan, or idea, often a written one
Objective	**d.** obtain goods or services from an outside supplier
Proposal	**e.** money paid extra for working after the usual time

2. **After meeting with the two representatives of the union in dialogue 6.1, Allen writes the following e-mail to the management committee. Complete the gaps with the correct form of the verbs below.**

> accept   be   give   meet   not be   receive   transfer

Dear Management Committee,

　　As you know, Edmund Brook and I _____ ① with the union representatives last night to discuss their rejection of the pay offer of 3%, effective 1 March and the threat of industrial action. Apart from the fact that white-collar workers _____ ② 5%, there _____ ③, as I suspected, strong rumours going around that we're closing the plant and _____ ④ work to France.

　　We _____ ⑤ the union representatives our reassurances that this _____ ⑥ the case and agreed on the 3% increase from 1 March, followed by a further 1.5% in nine months, as long as there _____ ⑦ a substantial fall in sales and provided that there is no industrial action. They _____ ⑧ the offer on behalf of their members.

　　We feel this is a successful conclusion to the negotiations.

Best wishes
Allen Macadam

3. **Work with a partner. Use the key words in brackets to make complete sentences about the conditions and offers below. The first sentence has been done for you.**

   1. Our members get 5% increase in pay/take industrial action (unless)

      Unless our members get a 5% increase in pay they will take industrial action.

   2. No further increase in pay/be no job losses Amsterdam (if/will)

      _____

   3. Another review in nine months/no industrial action (on condition that)

      _____

   4. Productivity increased/pay a bonus end of the year (if/could)

      _____

   5. Open on Sundays from 10 am—4 pm/lose business to competitors (unless)

      _____

V. OPTIONAL READING

How to Strike a Negotiable Opening Shot

There is no right or wrong ways to fire up your opening negotiation ...

There may be a lot of people who are uncertain about the right way to start off a fruitful negotiation with their counterparts. They tend to think or behave as though there is really a "right" way to start it off, which eventually will make them expect the magic  word "yes" from their opponent. There isn't any blueprint on how or what you should follow throughout your negotiation tactics, but perhaps there are several ways which you may want to consider.

Here are the 2 main important issues you need to consider when opening your negotiation talks.

a)   Hear, understand and tackle the main issues first and foremost.

b)   Build a cooperative environment and get the trust and respect from each other.

Say no to guerilla negotiating...

The first strategy is the most risky kind of tactic you shouldn't employ. If you demand too much in the first place, you may provoke and outrage the other opponent, which in the end may set your negotiations into a wrong direction. If things are so hard and difficult to come by for your opponent in the first place, do you think if by any chance that they will listen to you in the long run? They may not be aware of the significance of the main topics that you are bringing in, but tackling it later on will certainly save you a lot of time in the long run. Build rapport first.

Foster a closer relationship...

If things are too difficult to handle in the first place, the safest bet you can take on is to look for points at the outset that might bring you closer to your opponent. For example, try to get to know them well, have a small talk on their thoughts and principles and what are their likes and dislikes. This is something like an information gathering sessions, for what you've gathered may actually help you handle issues that are raised subsequently.

But you are advised to be cautious when using this tactic as the opponent may actually trying to outsmart you before they become more aggressive in the future. With this closer tie, try not to be too encouraged to give away information which you should not.

The final part...

Whatever tactics you may use for your opening negotiation, always try to give yourself an added advantage by kicking off the negotiation. You may be able to handle the proceedings well and to sum up matters which are more favorable to you.

Unit 7 Notice and Note

Unit Aims

- To know the form of notice and note
- To know how to write notice and note
- To master the basic expressions about notice and note
- To know some cultural background knowledge

Warming Up

Imagine you were a secretary of a company. Your company will hold an annual conference, which takes place every year in November. Please think about what kind of information is requested when inviting all the managers of each department to attend the meeting.

I. NOTICE

Both notice and announcement are written, printed or even oral statements which make the public know what has happened or will happen. For notice and announcement drafting, writers should pay attention to "what", "when", "where" and "whom", that is, what has happened or what will happen, when and where something has happened or will happen. Besides, to whom the information is given should be included. As far as language is concerned, it should be concise, simple, accurate and somewhat formal.

Unit 7 Notice and Note

1. Contents of Notice

Notice is usually used to give information, call meetings and arrange work. There are two types of notices: notices giving full message of information and notices giving a warning or an instruction.

Please read the following sample of notice and discuss the contents of the notice.

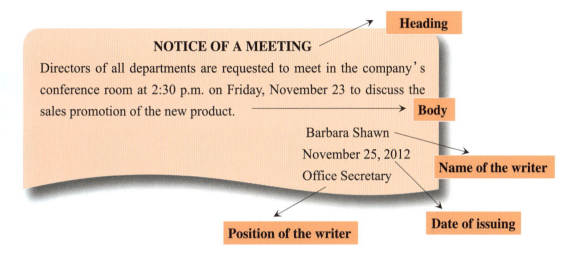

Contents of a Notice

A notice is usually made up of five parts:

1. **Heading:** It can help readers to focus on the purpose of the Notices as quickly as possible. It should be written all in capital letters.
2. **Body:** It is mainly about the information that is being conveyed.
3. **Signature:** Name of the person issuing the notice. It is usually put at the end of the body.
4. **Position:** of the person issuing the notice
5. **Date:** of the person issuing the notice or when the notice is written. The date appears below the signature, centered or in the bottom left-hand corner.

2. Layouts of Notice

Layout 1

Title

Body _____
_____

(Date)

Sample 1

NOTICE

    Notice is given that the New Year's Party of our company will be held at the room of Company Committee Club on the tenth floor of our headquarters on 28 December.

December 20th, 2012

Layout 2

Date

Salutation,
Body _____
_____
_____
_____.

Close
Signature

Sample 2

December 10th, 2012

Dear Sir/Madam,

    Owing to the large increase of our trade in this region, we have decided to open a branch here, with Mr. Zhao Liang as manager. The new branch will open on 1st of January and from that date, all orders and inquiries should be sent to Mr. Zhao Liang. We show our great thanks for your cooperation in the past. We are longing for the new cooperation.

Yours,
Li Xiao

Layout 3

To:
From:
Date:
Subject:
Body _____
_____
_____

Sample 3

To: All Staff
From: Board of Directors
Date: December 7, 2012
Subject: Appointment of a new manager

    Owing to the large increase of our trade in this region, we have decided to open a branch here. With the new branch opening, we need a manager to operate it. After 3 months' consideration, we have decided to appoint Mr. Zhao Liang as the new manager. We hope you will make efforts to support him to make our company better in the future.

3. Types of Notice

Notices may be released in many different ways, such as posted up on notice board or bulletin board, advertised on the newspaper, or sent as a letter or an e-mail. According to the ways they are released, they usually can be divided into four forms: form of poster; form of leaflet; form of mail or letter and notice as public signs.

Type 1: Poster Notices

The language of poster notices should be short and simple. It should include information on what, when and where.

BASKETBALL Match
Production Department team
vs.
Sales Department team
4:30 p.m., Friday, May 15, 2002
Southern District Gymnasium
Get your tickets (10 RMB) from May Long in Staff Relations!!

Type 2: Leaflet Notices

A leaflet notice contains more information and is often used as a way of promotion. Readers can use this form (once filled in) to receive a special offer such as a discount or a present.

The Opening of Jiuzhou Supermarket

We are pleased to announce that Jiuzhou Supermarket will be opened on December 25. It is a special supermarket for the customers at Lanshan District.

High quality goods will be supplied at reasonable prices, and much effort will be made to provide our customers with an enjoyable shopping environment.

To mark this special occasion, customers will be able to take advantage of a free membership card and enjoy 10% reduction on the price of your purchase.

Type 3: Letter Notices

A mail or letter notice can be especially useful for giving information about complex events as it is not limited by the format. In the letter or mail notices, the voice should be passive, the tone should be positive, and the sentences should be imperative.

December 10th, 2012

Dear Sir/Madam,

Owing to the large increase of our trade in this region, we have decided to open a branch here, with Mr. Zhao Liang as manager. The new branch will open on 1st of January and from that date, all orders and inquiries should be sent to Mr. Zhao Liang.

We show our great thanks for your cooperation in the past.

We are longing for the new cooperation.

Yours,
Li Xiao

Unit 7　Notice and Note

Type 4: Public Signs Notices
There are three kinds of public signs notices:
1) Signs forbidding or obligating a certain action(s).
2) Signs for warning.
3) Signs giving information or direction.

Samples of the three kinds are as follows:
1) Signs forbidding or obligating a certain action(s).

> Don't Touch High-Voltage Wire. Don't Dump Rubbish Here. No Smoking, Offender to Be Fined 10 Dollars

2) Signs for warning.

> Reduce Speed Now
> Be Careful
> Keep Away from Heat
> Beware of Dogs

3) Signs giving information or direction.

> Office Hour: 8:30 a.m.—17:00 p.m.
> Not for Sale
> This Way to the Toilet
> Please Pay in Cash
> Turn Left

4. Useful Phrases and Expressions

Notice is hereby given that ...
This is to notify that ...
We inform you that ...
I have the pleasure of announcing that ...
There will be a ...(meeting) at... (time) in/at...(place)
I am pleased to tell you that...
I am writing to inform you that...
Please informed that...
I/ we have pleasure in informing you that...
I'd like to tell you that...
All the staff members are expected at the meeting.

5. Practicing

1. Complete the notice with the following expressions.

| a number of activities | ranked | are preparing to |
| are welcome | with the efforts of | |

NOTICE

We (1)_____ celebrate the 20th anniversary of our company. (2)_____ all our staff, our company has been in the present situation, (3)_____ as one of the leading companies in the field of electrical appliances in our country. In order to show thanks and encourage all the employees, we will hold (4)_____. The employees' suggestions and proposals (5)_____ and those being accepted will be awarded. Please hand in your proposals to our office or e-mail your proposals to SUNJ@126.com.

If you still have any questions, please telephone the office at XXXXXXXX.

The Manager Office

2. Pease write notice according to the following information.

1)

通　知

本周五(12月14)下午2:30各部门经理在公司会议室902房间召开本季度销售总结会议,请准时出席。

行政办

2012年12月11日

2)

Suppose you are a secretary of a company, now it is the end of the year, and the General Manager will hold a year-end sales meeting. You are required to write a meeting notice which should include the following issues:

Time: 8:30 a.m.—17:30 p.m. Dec. 28th

Place: Head Office Meeting Room

To: All staff

Lunch Provided

You may think about the other matters that are included in the notice.

Unit 7　Notice and Note

II. NOTE

1. Format of a Note

Every note is made up of five essential parts, including heading, salutation, body, closing and signature. They comprise the structure or framework of your note. You should follow the general form if you want to produce a correct and acceptable note.

Heading	Date
Salutation (use colon or comma)	Dear _____ :
Body	_____ _____ _____ _____ _____ _____
Closing	Sincerely,
Signature	Signature

2. Language Style of a Note

The important points of note writing for attention are clearness, conciseness, coherence, correctness, completeness, and courtesy.

1) Clearness

　　Note writing should be unambiguous and clear enough for addressees to catch its meaning but not to misunderstand it. With the proper expression and simplicity of phrases and sentence structures, you can make your note writing well understood.

　　Unclear: Mr. Wang wrote to Mr. He that he had accepted his plan.

　　Clear: Mr. Wang wrote to Mr. He that he had accepted Mr. He's plan.

2) Conciseness

　　A good writing can make addressees obtain more information from your notes within less time. Writing should be read fluently and be concise so that it can catch addressees' attention.

Redundant: In your previous letter, you enquired about our experience with Mr. Li. We are happy to tell you about his work for us. He was a loyal and faithful worker during the three years he worked as a secretary.

Concise: Mr. Li about whom you enquired in your previous letter had been a loyal secretary here for three years.

3) Coherence

Coherence of writing is very important. You can express the complete meaning of a note with logic connection between sentences. When writing a note, you should pay attention to the coherence of subject, voice, tense, and tone.

Incoherent: Your organization had been more than just a small company. It was an institution in the minds of the Chinese public. It has a reputation for honesty with both employees and customers.

Coherent: Your organization is more than just a small company. It is an institution in the minds of the Chinese public. It has a reputation for honesty with both employees and customers.

4) Correctness

In your writing, you should give definite and correct information so as not to make it misunderstood. If your information is not given correctly, the addressee will feel puzzled about what he is going to do.

Incorrect: I'd like to invite you to my birthday party this Saturday, at 7 o'clock.

Correct: I'd like to invite you to my birthday party on this Saturday evening, December 15, at 7 o'clock.

5) Completeness

The content of your writing should be complete. If you ignore some necessary details, your writing will affect social activities and make addressees disappointed. If you beat about the bush in your writing, addressees will be bored and confused. However, if the writing is too simple and brief, it can not achieve the purpose for communication and business dealings.

Incomplete: Here is the time, date, and plane information for your trip to Beijing: You will fly Western Suburbs Air Lines on next Thursday.

Complete: Your reservation are for next Thursday, December 20th, on Western Suburbs Airlines Flight #215, leaving Jinan at 9:10 a.m. for Beijing.

6) Courtesy

Last but not least, courtesy is necessary. Although courtesy can not help you achieve the purpose of writing, it can express your politeness and show your respect to addressees.

Discourteous: Interview me whenever you want.

Unit 7　Notice and Note

Courteout: If you desire an interview, I shall be most happy to call in person, on any day and at any time you may appoint.

III. TYPES OF NOTES

Notes can be classified into many types according to different purposes such as invitation, apology, appointment, thank-you, borrowing, asking for leave etc. The following part will just exemplify several useful ones.

1) Note of Appointment

A schedule plays a very important role in people's work and life, so a note of appointment is necessary if we want to visit some people on some occasions. If we make an appointment with someone, a note should include our request and reasons, the available date, the time, the place, our address or telephone number, and appreciation for his concern.

> Dear Lucy,
>
> 　　Paul is going to New York tomorrow morning to pursue his graduate study and we will not be able to see him for a long time. We will have a dinner party at 6:30 p.m. this evening at his home. It would be nice if you could come with us.
>
> 　　　　　　　　　　　　　　　　　　　　　　　　　　Yours,
> 　　　　　　　　　　　　　　　　　　　　　　　　　　Lisa

Useful phrases when writing notes of appointment

I will be glad to meet with you in ...... on ......, to discuss our project.

If you are unable to make the meeting on ......, please let me know as soon as possible.

I would appreciate thirty minutes of your time this week to discuss our cooperation.

I'll give you a call in a couple of days to see if you can schedule an appointment with me.

2) Note of Thanks

A note of thanks is written when someone renders a special service, or when you have been someone's guest. Commercial thank-you notes are not acceptable.

> Dear Mr. Wang,
>
> 　　I am writing to express my heartfelt appreciation for all that you did for me in my project. It is very kind of you to have spared me such a long time to help me to finish my design. Now I'm happy to learn that my design has been passed, which, I understand clearly, should be attributed to your generous help. Heartfelt thanks again.
>
> 　　　　　　　　　　　　　　　　　　　　　　　　　Sincerely yours,
> 　　　　　　　　　　　　　　　　　　　　　　　　　Sophia

Useful phrases when writing notes of thanks

Thank you very much for the...

I am writing to tell you how grateful I was for the...

I cannot thank you enough for the...

I am writing to express my appreciation for all that you have done for ...

Everything seemed perfect with your consideration.

I hope I have the chance to return your kindness.

3) Note of Congratulation

The note of congratulation must be written, especially to congratulate people who have accomplished things. We express feelings of pleasure and shared excitement when people are the recipients of life's bounties.

March. 22

Dear Robert,

   I learned about your promotion from John. Congratulations! It certainly is not easy for you to have this chance to be promoted. So it is nice to know that hard work and intelligence is still recognized.

   All of us who know you here know how hard you have strived and how bright you are. You make us all proud of you!

Sincerely yours,

Levis

Useful phrases when writing notes of congratulations

Please accept my heartiest congratulations on ......

Your considerate arrangement and patient companionship made my trip very joyful. Hearty congratulations and all good wishes on ......

Congratulations and best wishes to you.

Best luck to you, now and in the future.

4) Note of Apology

Occasionally, when we do something embarrassing, the only solution is a note of apology. A note of apology is the need of courtesy to avoid misunderstanding and offence.

Dear Cindy,

   I'd like to express my apologies for not being able to take part in your birthday party, for it happens to be my turn to be on duty and will have to work till 11 o'clock this evening. Happy birthday to you! May every day be sunny for you in the coming year!

                                                        Yours,

                                                        Lucy

Useful phrases when writing notes of apology

I am terribly/very sorry/extremely embarrassed/ most upset about my behavior last night.

I (do) apologize for ....

Please accept my sincere apologies for my inattention/ thoughtlessness/shortsightedness.

Sadly, I regret to say that I hurt you inattentively.

Unfortunately, I'm afraid I can't fulfill what you ask me to do.

I am not excusing my errors, but I hope you can forgive me.

I promise that I will remedy my mistake.

I hope to / to be able to compensate you for loss.

I will make certain/assure you that this doesn't happen again.

5) Note of Invitation

    A note of invitation is an invitation to actions as the following: to visit a place; to attend an event; to make a contribution and so on. Occasionally notes of invitation are not unnecessarily formal in their writing.

                                                        December 20

Dear Lisa,

    We are planning Christmas party and we want you to come. It's December 25, at 7 o'clock in the evening.

    I do hope that you can make it, as all of us are looking forward with great pleasure to seeing you.

                                                        Yours,

                                                        Rosemary

Useful phrases when writing notes of invitation

We are wondering if you could come to ...

We would like to invite you to ...

We are hoping that you can take part in ...

We have the honor of inviting...

I am looking forward to seeing you.

We hope nothing will prevent you from coming, as we are waiting for your visit.

It will be so good to see you again.

IV. PRACTICING

Please write notes according to the following directions:

1) Directions:

You are Mary, and you have been entertained as a house guest at the home of a friend, Amelia. Write a note of thanks to her mother, Mrs. Walton.

2) Directions:

Your boss, the sales manager, has just been promoted to be the general manager of your company. Please write a congratulation note to express your pleasure at his recognition of his worth.

V. OPTIONAL READING

Business Thank-You Etiquette

The handwritten thank-you note is perhaps the most underused and misused form of follow-up marketing that exists today. At the completion of this article, you will both understand how to effectively write a thank-you note and why it is important.

The "Why"

Writing a thank-you note is conscientious and caring. The implied message from the recipient is that you sat down and took time to write and think only about them at that moment. It is subliminal but understood. Most people personally dislike the act of writing thank-you notes, so when they get one, they appreciate the time dedication you took for them.

It will actually be read. Most generic forms of follow-up are easily identifiable and discarded into the trash without being opened. But when people receive a handwritten thank-you note with a handwritten address on the envelope, they open it.

It's a reminder. People often visit many different locations before making a purchase, so they may not actually remember you. The thank-you note is a reminder that the person did come visit you and the experience was a good one. Many times, the person may still not remember you specifically, but the thank-you makes them "think" they enjoyed what you had, so they will come out a second time.

The "How"

Always handwrite the thank-you note. The handwritten thank-you is the purest, oldest and most understood form of appreciation. Most of your competitors send generic or automated type letters. Be different. In today's world of automation, the handwritten thank-you note is dying more and more each day. Make the commitment, stay the course, and reap the benefits.

Do not list your credentials or boast about your company. Recount a detail from your encounter. Jog the person's memory to create a visualization that only you and that person shared.

This also displays a level of confidence that you feel the meeting went well. It affirms to the prospect that you believe in your product and yourself. And it subtly relays that the prospect also enjoyed the encounter. If you thought it went poorly, would you be writing to remind them about it?

Be sure to conclude a short message with a clearly readable name and phone number. Never assume the person already has your information.

The Benefits

With your new understanding of the tremendous value thank-you cards, you will begin to reap the benefits. These will come in the form of an increased capture ratio because you will have more second appointments. You will have more clients thanking you for your notes to them, and you will deliver better presentations to clients because you will pay closer attention if you are going to write an effective thank-you note.

(http://www.ehow.com/way_5218816_business-thank-etiquette.html)

Unit 8 Business Letters

Unit Aims

- To know the form and layout of business letters
- To master the basic expressions about business letters
- To know how to write the business letters
- To know the etiquette of writing business letters

Warming Up

Nadine Beck is a personal assistant at Quantum, a small consulting firm in Berlin. Her responsibilities include managing the office and dealing with her boss's correspondence. Imagine you are Nadine Beck and using the following channels in certain situation of office communication.

What would you use to do?
- Order some equipment?
- Resign from your job?
- Tell the staff about a colleague's going-away party?
- Get some details from a customer or business partner?
- Inform everybody in your department of an important meeting?
- Send a contract?
- Tell your boss that you're going to be late?
- Applying for a job?

Unit 8　Business Letters

Situations	Channels
Order some equipment	
resign from your job	
tell staff about a going-away party	
get details from a customer	

Channels: *telephoning, face to face, video conference, letter, text message, etc.*

I. PARTS OF A BUSINESS LETTER

1. Letterhead

The letterhead provides the sender's name, full address, the telephone number, fax number, cable address and e-mail address.

2. Inside address

The inside address shows who the letter is to.

3. Reference and Date

Reference is used when one company writes to another, which may be a file number, a departmental code and etc.

There is no standard way of writing the date in English, but this form is now by far the most common in modern business letters: 1 December 2012.

4. Salutation

If you know the name of the person who will deal with your letter, then use it, e.g. Dear xxx or Dear Mr xxx. In business letters, always use the neutral form Ms for women unless the woman herself uses Mrs or Miss. If you don't know the person's name, use the impersonal form Dear Sir or Madam. Do not use a comma.

5. Subject Line (事由)

The subject line says what the letter is about in a few key words. It is generally written in bold letters or underlined, e.g. **Enquiry** or Inquiry.

6. Complimentary close (信尾敬语)

Always finish your letter with a complimentary close. If you begin with a name, e.g. Dear Ms Cindy, then close with Yours sincerely. If you begin with Dear Sir or Madam, then close with

Yours faithfully. Do not use a comma.

7. Signature block

The signature block shows that the letter is from a company, not from a private person. The full company name comes before the writer's signature. When writing to a company for the first time, the writer also gives his or her position in the company, e.g. General Manager.

8. Copies

The letters cc mean carbon copy. They show the addressee who else in the sender's company has received a copy of the letter.

9. Enclosure(s)

If you have put something else in the envelope with the letter, then say no and add Enc for one item or Encs for two or more items.

Here is a sample of the general position of these parts.

APEX
CONSUMER DATA LTD······ **1. Letterhead**
30 Docklands Road
London A3 6JH
Tel+55-717-667399-0 Fax+5555-717-667399-0
Internet www.acd.co.uk Email info@acd.co.uk
Registered in England VAT No.387/316

Old Manor Hotel
25 Riverside
Horning
RN12 8P L······ **2. Inside address**

Our ref: HC/TS
Your ref:······ **3.Reference**
23 November 2012······ **3.Date**

Dear Sir or Madam,······ **4. Salutation**
Conference facilities······ **5. Subject Line**

　　We were interested to read your advertisement in the October edition of *Training Matters*.

　　As you will see from the enclosed image brochure, Apex Consumer Data is one of the biggest market research companies in the UK.

　　One important reason for our success is our intensive 2-day training seminars for interviewers and call center staff, which we like to hold in quiet country locations.

We would be grateful if you could send us details of your conference facilities and prices. We are particularly interested in your weekend rates (Friday evening to Sunday evening) and in your special winter rates.

Thank you for your trouble, and we look forward to hearing from you soon.

Yours faithfully······ **6. Complimentary close**
Apex Consumer Data Ltd
Nadine Beck······ **7. Signature block**
Nadine Beck
Training Manager
cc: Harry Webb, Planning······ **8. Copies**
Enc: company image brochure······ **9. Enclosure(s)**

II. BASIC PRINCIPLES OF WRITING A BUSINESS LETTER

There are seven principles of writing business letters. Generally, these principles are called "Seven-C's". They are completeness, conciseness, consideration, concreteness, clarity, courtesy and correctness. Here are the "seven C's" in detail:

1. **COMPLETENESS:** This means the business message must contain all the facts the reader or listener needs for the reaction you desire. You must provide necessary information and give something extra if desired or needed.
2. **CONCISENESS:** Eliminate wordy expressions and include material that is relevant. Also, avoid unnecessary repetition.
3. **CONSIDERATION:** Focus on 'you' attitude instead of 'I' and 'we' attitude. But then overuse of it might lead to a negative reaction.
4. **CONCRETENESS:** Whenever possible use specific facts and figures and use active verbs in order to make your message more precise.
5. **CLARITY:** Construct effective sentences and paragraphs.
6. **COURTSEY:** Use expressions that show respect and be sincerely tactful, thoughtful and appreciative.
7. **CORRECTNESS:** Use the right level of language and also maintain acceptable writing mechanics.

III. BASIC PHRASES AND EXPRESSIONS

Read the following dialogue and talk about the key phrases and sentences when writing a business letter.

Scott: Can you help me for a minute?

Hunter: Sure, what can I do for you?

Scott: I'm trying to write a letter to one of our clients, but I just don't know exactly what to say. I don't even know how to get started. I know I should write dear Mr., Mrs. or Ms., but the problem is I don't know the name of the contact person.

Hunter: You can just put "Dear Sir or Madam," official not personal. You can also write "To whom it may concern."

Scott: OK, so I first thank them for their business. I can say something like "We are very grateful for your continuous support." How is that?

Hunter: Good! But also, you need to tell them the reason of your writing, give them more reference.

Scott: Like "Regarding our new product line, we would like to announce a special price discount."

Hunter: Right, do you need them to respond?

Scott: Yes, the letter would have a survey inside, and they should complete it and return to our office. How should I write that?

Hunter: You can tell them "Please find the enclosed customer service survey," else also, you can say: "Attach a customer survey." If you need resource it right away, you can tell them the urgent by saying "Please return the survey without delay as soon as possible. Maybe it is more polite with this as early as convenient."

Scott: Great! And what do you think I should close it with?

Hunter: Since you don't know them that well personally, probably the best way would be yours or your sincerely. You can also say Best Regards. But I don't think it would be proper because you don't have the name. And obviously, you should have them.

Scott: OK. Thanks a lot for your help!

Unit 8 Business Letters

Key Phrases and Expressions for a Business Letter

Dear Sir or Madam

Thank you for your letter of 23 November.

We are writing to inform you that the meeting on November 25 had been canceled.

We kindly request that you send your RSVP as soon as possible.

We'd be grateful if you could...

We apologize for any inconvenience this may cause.

You will find the new agenda enclosed/as an attachment.

Please contact me if you have any questions...

If we can be of further assistance, please do not hesitate to contact us.

I look forward to hearing from you.

Yours faithfully/sincerely

IV. SAMPLES OF BUSINESS LETTERS

1. Specific Enquiry Letter

Opening	If you are writing to a company for the first time, say where you got the firm's name and address and who you are. If you are writing to a company you already do business with, start with giving a reason for the enquiry.
Reason	Always say why you are making the enquiry. It can also be quite useful to give brief background information here.
Request	Say what you want the addressee to do. Make sure that you include all the necessary details. If you have any questions about discounts or delivery, for example, ask them here.
Close	Make a polite and friendly closing comment that motivates the addressee to answer your enquiry promptly.

A Model Letter

Robert Dorn is a purchasing manager with ProVitesse Kosemetika GmbH, a cosmetics wholesaler in London. In this enquiry, Robert Dorn asks Plant Bodycare Ltd in London to send him an offer of a trial consignment of hair gels and shampoo.

ProVitesse

Kosmetika GmbH

Landauer Weg 17. D-50233 London.　　　Tel+47-233-754406 .Fax+47-233-754406

Mail: info@provitesse.de Website: www.provitesse.de

Your ref: _____　　　　　　　　　Our ref: HH/A2

Plant Bodycare Ltd

35 Nelson Road

London A5 6AX

England

25 October 2012

Dear Ms Adam,

Enquiry

Further to my visit to your stand at the Cosmetics Fair in Brussels, we are very interested in selling your range of haircare products here in England.

We would, therefore, be grateful if you could send us a firm offer for a trial consignment of the following lines:

1. 5 (five) cases Adona hair gel, Oder No. HG1693, 24 boxed tubes per case
2. 4 (four) cases FixUp extre gel, Oder No. HG1774, 24 boxed tubes per case
3. 4 (four) cases Medex shampoo, Oder No. SM2091, 24 boxed bottles per case

As agreed in Brussels, please quote DDP our London stores on your usual trade terms. As we are sure that your products could be a big seller here, we look forward to receiving your offer soon.

Yours sincerely

ProVitesse Kosemetika GmbH

Robert Dorn

Robert Dorn

Purchasing Manager, Haircare

Useful Phrases for Enquiry

Opening

We were invited to read/see your advertisement in ...of ...

When we visited your website, we were interested to see that you ...

We prefer to your entry in ...that ...

You have been recommended to us by ..., who told us that you ...

Unit 8 Business Letters

Reasoning

When we visited your stand at ..., we were interested to hear that you ...

We are looking for a supplier of ...

At present we have extended our range of ..., and ...

Request

We would be grateful if you could quote us for ...

Please send us an offer for the following products ...

All prices should be ...

Please send us ... samples of ... for our inspection.

Close

We look forward to receiving your offer/quotation in due course/soon.

Thank you in advance for your assistance/help.

We hope to hear from you in due course.

2. An offer Letter

You write offers (or quotations) in answer to enquiries about specific products. Enquiries have three or four parts, as follows:

Opening	Refer to the original enquiry, with date and product line.
Details	Give clear and complete details of quantity, packing, product, order number and price. Except for price, take these from the enquiry. If possible, use a table.
Terms	Give information about delivery, discounts and terms of payment.
Close	Thank the firm for their enquiry and ask them to contact you if they have any questions. You can also say that you are looking forward to an order.

A Model Letter

This is Jane Adam's reply to Robert Dorn's specific enquiry.

	PLANT
	Bodycare Limited
ProVitesse Kosmetika GmbH	Your ref: HH/A2
Landauer Weg 17	Our ref: YH/sw/1
D-50233 London	
England	
	10 November 2012

Dear Mr Dorn,

OFFER

Thank you very much for your enquiry of 25 October, and we would be happy to supply you on the following terms:

1. 5 (five) cases Adona hair gel, HG1693	€ 216.00/case	€ 1080
2. 3 (three) cases FixUp extra gel, HG1774	€ 240.00/case	€ 720
3. 4 (four) cases Medex shampoo, SM2091	€ 72.00/case	€ 288
	Total Invoice price	€ 2088

As requested, all prices are DDP your London stores for immediate delivery.

As agreed in Brussels, these prices are 10% below trade price for a first order. We also offer a further cash discount of 2% for payment in full received within 15 days of delivery.

Thank you again for enquiry and please contact us if you have any questions.

We look forward to receiving an order from you.

Your sincerely
PLANT Bodycare Limited

Jane Adam
Jane Adam
Export Department

cc: John Carr, Marking
35 Nelson Road London A5 6Ax
Tel+47-233-754406 Fax+47-223-754406
E-mail info@plant.co.uk
Website www.plant.co.uk
Registered in England Vat No.79522

Unit 8　Business Letters

Useful Phrases for an Offer Letter

Opening

Thank you (very much) for your enquiry of ...

With reference to your enquiry/our telephone conversation of...

Details

We are pleased to make the following offer/quotation:...

We should be happy to supply you with the following products:...

Terms

We are willing to offer you the following terms of delivery/payment:...

...a/an introductory/trade/volume discount of...% off/on list price.

...a cash discount of 2% for payment within...days.

All prices are EXW/CIF Tilbury.

We expect payment on our usual terms and conditions of business.

Payment should be made with...days of receipt of goods/invoice.

Delivery will be made on...

The consignment/goods will be dispatched on...

Close

Thank you again for your enquiry.

We are certain that you will be (completely) satisfied with our products.

If you have any questions, please contact me on...

We look forward to receiving your order in due course.

3. An Order Letter

Parts of an order letter.

Opening	Refer to the offer and say that you wish to place an order.
Details	Specify your order (quantity, produce, number, type, price, etc.).
Terms	Confirm the terms and conditions (specify a date for delivery).
Close	Close with a polite phrase.

A Model Letter

Robert Dorn is satisfied with Plant Bodycare's offer (a model letter of an offer), so he places a trial order. Note that he repeats the most important information again.

ProVitesse

Kosmetika Gmbh

Landauer Weg 17. D-50233 London.   Tel+47-233-754406 .Fax+47-233-754406
Mail: info@provitesse.de   Website: www.provitesse.de
Your ref:YH/sw/1   Our ref:HH/A2

Plant Bodycare Ltd
35 Nelson Road
London A5 6Ax
England

18 November 2012

Dear Ms Adam

Order No.1/HK/NB

Thank you for your offer of 10 November, and we should like to place a trial order for the following items at the prices you quote:

We would, therefore, be grateful if you could sent us a firm offer for a trial consignment of the following lines:

1. 5(five) cases Adina hair gel, HG1693   € 216.00/case   € 1080
2. 3(three) cases FixUp extra gel, HG1774   € 240.00/case   € 720
3. 4(four) cases Medex shampoo, SM2091   € 72.00/case   € 288

We note that all prices are DDP our London stores and are 10% below trade price. We also note that you are willing to allow us a further cash discount of 2% for full payment received within 15 days of delivery.

Thank you for dealing with our enquiry so promptly, and we look forward to receiving the consignment soon.

Yours sincerely

Robert Dorn
Robert Dorn
Purchasing Manager, Haircare

Useful Phrases for an Order Letter

Opening

Many thanks for your current catalogue/price-list.

Thank you for sending us /letting us have your offer.

Thank you for your offer of ... /we have received your offer of ...

Unit 8　Business Letters

We have carefully examined/tested your samples/specimens.
We are pleased with both the quality of your samples and your prices.

Details: placing an order

We should like to place the following order, ...
Please supply the following products: ...
We refer to/with reference to your offer of ... (and) (we)would like to place the following order:
Having looked at the samples/specimens you sent us, we wish to order the following (for immediate delivery).
Our order is based on your catalogue number. ..
Please find enclosed/we enclose our order, number 8765, for the following items: ...

Delivery Terms

We note that these prices include an introductory/a trade/volume discount of ...% off/on list price
We understand that you are willing to give/allow us a cash discount of ...%
Payment will be made ... immediately on delivery/receipt of the consignment/goods.
...within ... days of receipt of your invoice.
We note that the consignment will be dispatched by ... on ...
The goods ordered must be delivered immediately.
We must insist that the goods be supplied within ten days.
If you are unable to/if you cannot deliver within this period ...
Delivery should be Franco domicile.
We accept your terms of payment and delivery.

Close

Please confirm the above order as soon as possible.
Please acknowledge receipt of this order.
Thank you in advance and we look forward to receiving the consignment by.../shortly.

4. An Acknowledgment Letter

You should acknowledge receipt of all orders. Parts of the acknowledgment letter are as follows.

Opening	Thank the customer for an order
Details	Say what you expect
Close	Close with a polite phrase

A Model Letter

Here, Jane Adam of Plant Bodycare acknowledges receipt of the trial order from Provitesse. Apart from confirming the details of the original offer, this also gives her the chance to thank ProVitesse for their order again.

Plant Bodycare Limited
35 Nelson Road London A5 6Ax
Tel+44-171-709-303-0
Fax+44-171-709-303-22
E-mail info @ plant .co.uk
Website www.plant.co.uk
Registered in England Vat No.79522

Dear Mr Done

    We acknowledge receipt of your order No. 1/HK/NB on the terms quoted in our offer of 10 November.

    Thank you very much for your order, and we are sure that you will be completely satisfied with our products.

Yours sincerely

Jane Adam

cc:Joshua Clarke, Logistics

Useful Phrases for an Acknowledgements Letter

Opening

Many thanks/thank you for your order for ... of ...

We are pleased to acknowledge receipt of your order for ... of ...

We acknowledge/confirm receipt of your order/your order No. ... of ...

Details

We are pleased to confirm the terms of payment and delivery as stated in your order.

We confirm the terms of your order as follows: ...

Please note that the consignment will be dispatched on ...

We will inform you (by fax/phone/email) as soon as the goods have left our factory/stores.

We hope/expect that the consignment/order will leave our stores/plant in ... on ...

Close

We would like to thank you for the order/for your confidence in our products.

If there are any problems, please contact me/us immediately.

We are sure/convinced that you will be completely satisfied with our products and service.

V. PRACTICING

1. Please use the numbers 1–4 to link the salutations to a suitable complimentary close, a–d.

1) Dear Sir or Madam   a. Yours
2) Dear Ruther   b. Yours sincerely
3) Ladies and Gentlemen   c. Yours faithfully
4) Dear Ms Martin   d. Very truly yours

2. Link the definitions 1–8 with parts of a business letter a–h

1) A company's name, address etc. printed at the top of a letter.	a. body
2) Information on what the letter is about.	b. complimentary close
3) The addressee's full address.	c. inside address
4) The reference of the original letter.	d. letterhead
5) The polite expression that begins a business letter.	e. salutation
6) The polite expression that finishes a business letter.	f. signature block
7) The text of a business letter.	g. subject line
8) The writer's company, signature, name and position at the end of a business letter.	h. Your reference:

3. Put the sentences of this enquiry into the correct order.

1) As a supplier of football equipment and clothing, we are currently expanding our range and wish to start supplying women's wear as well as men's wear.

2) Dear Sir or Madam

3) Purchasing Manager

4) Thank you in advance for your help.

5) We look forward to hearing from you soon.

6) We saw your advertisement in the June issue of "Fashion World" and were particularly interested by your range of sportswear.

7) Yours faithfully

8) We would also appreciate information about volume and trade discounts.

9) Jane Adams

10) We would, therefore, be very grateful if you could send us a copy of your brochure, as well as an up-to-date price list.

4. Combine the verbs in group A with the appropriate nouns in group B.

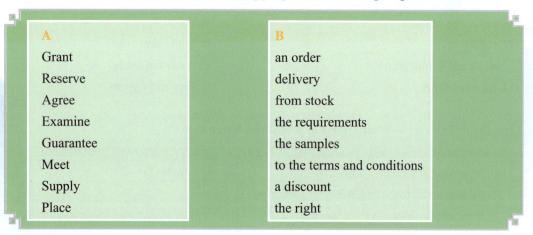

A	B
Grant	an order
Reserve	delivery
Agree	from stock
Examine	the requirements
Guarantee	the samples
Meet	to the terms and conditions
Supply	a discount
Place	the right

5. Writing letters

Please use the material in the box to complete the enquiry about exercise cycles for fitness studios.

Opening
- Express interest in products, refer to an advertisement in "Health and Fitness World" magazine.
- Background information, reason for enquiry
- You are Munich-based fitness-centre chain
- You are particularly interested in exercise cycles "ProMedic"

Request
- Ask for a representative to call, as well as price-lists and terms of business
- Also appreciate information about discounts

Close
- Thank addressee for their trouble
- Look forward to hearing from them

VI. OPTIONAL READING

Business Letter Etiquette

Business etiquette is fundamentally concerned with building relationships founded upon courtesy and politeness between business personnel. Etiquette, and especially business etiquette, is a means of maximising your potential by presenting yourself positively.

The foundation of good business letter etiquette is "Think before you write". You should be considering who the letter is addressed to, how and why? This will then influence style, content and structure.

Addressing the Letter

Always make sure you have spelt the recipient's name correctly. It may sound simple, but you would be surprised at how many people fail to do so. The recipient's name should include titles, honours or qualifications if deemed necessary.

Many people use the 'Dear Sir/Yours Faithfully' formula when addressing the receiver. Although this is acceptable for routine matters, it is impersonal and should not be used when dealing with those you know, queries or complaints. With these the 'Dear Mr. ... /Yours Sincerely' formula should be adopted.

Style

Proper business letter etiquette requires that a consistent and clear approach, combined with courtesy, be employed. As a rule of thumb, aim to keep all business letters formal in style. Even when the receiver is familiar to you, it is advisable to maintain a certain level of business etiquette as the letter may be seen by others or referred to by a third party in the future.

However, this does not mean you should use long or uncommon words to express yourself. This merely looks odd and makes the letter unreadable. It is best to read a letter first and consider whether you would speak to that person face to face in the same way. If not, then rewrite it.

Letters should be signed personally. It looks unprofessional, cold and somewhat lazy if a letter is left unsigned. However, having a secretary or PA sign on your behalf is not considered a breach of business etiquette.

Humour

Humour can be used in business letters but only when the writer is completely positive that the recipient will understand the joke or pun. From a business etiquette perspective it may be wise to avoid humour. This is because firstly, the letter may be read during a crisis, after receiving bad news or on a somber occasion. Any other time the humour may have been appreciated but under these circumstances it may dramatically backfire. Secondly, the written word is open to misinterpretation. Your sarcastic or ironic remark may be taken the wrong way. Thirdly, it is possible that the letter may be read by a third party who may deem the humour inappropriate and pursue a complaint of some sort.

Responding

Good business letter etiquette calls for letters to be responded to promptly or within certain guidelines. This may normally be considered as 5 working days. If this is not possible then some sort of acknowledgement should be sent either by letter, fax, phone or e-mail.

Always use reference numbers or clearly state the purpose of the letter at the top, for example, 'Re: Business Letter Etiquette Enquiry'. This allows the receiver to trace correspondence and immediately set your letter within a context.

When replying to points or questions the proper etiquette is to respond in the same order as they were asked.

Unit 9 Business Travel

Unit Aims

- To know how to check in/out in a hotel
- To know how to make an airline reservation
- To master the basic expressions about business travel
- To know some cultural background knowledge about business travel

Warming Up

It is your first day as a receptionist in Shangri-la hotel. And you are preparing a list of English phrases to help you as a receptionist. What other phrases can you add to the list?

Would you please sign here?
How long do you plan to stay?
Could you please spell your name?

I. CHECK IN

Read the following two conversations between the guest and the receptionist.

Conversation 1:

Guest: Hi, I'm here to check in.
Receptionist: You must be Mr. Adams.
Guest: Yes, that's right.
Receptionist: Welcome to our hotel. Would you please fill out this registration form?
Receptionist: Thank you ...Excuse me, sir. You forgot to fill in your visa number.
Guest: Did I? Let me see that...Oh, sorry...Here you are.
Receptionist: And would you sign here, please? Thank you. May I see your passport, please? Thank you. Would you mind leaving your passport here for an hour or so? We must make a copy of your passport and visa for our records.
Receptionist: I'm sorry, your visa has expired.
Guest: What? You're kidding! Let me see that...There must be some mistake. I don't understand how that could be.
Receptionist: I'm afraid you'll need to go to the Public Security Bureau to have your visa extended before we can have you check in. It's not far from here. A taxi can take you there in five minutes.

Conversation 2:

Guest: Hi. I have a reservation for tonight, and I just want to check in.
Receptionist: Sure. What's your name?
Guest: Uh. Mike Adams.
Receptionist: Okay. Let me check here. Um. Here's your key card. You're in room 360. Just walk down this hall, and you'll see the elevators on your right.
Guest: Oh, okay, and what time is the restaurant open for breakfast?
Receptionist: It serves breakfast from 6:30-10 a.m.
Guest: Oh, okay. And, uh, where's the exercise room? I'd like to run a couple of miles before going to bed tonight.
Receptionist: It's on the second floor, and it's open till 10 tonight.
Guest: Oh, oh well. And one final question. Do you have wireless Internet in the rooms?
Receptionist: We DO [Ah!]... for $7.95 a night.
Guest: Ahhhh. I thought something like that

would be included in the price of the room.
Receptionist: Sorry, sir.
Guest: Ahhhh. What's my room again?
Receptionist: Three sixty (360).
Guest: Thank you.

II. CHECK OUT

Read the following dialogue and talk about why the caller need to change the appointment?

Conversation 1:
Guest: I'd like to check out.
Receptionist: Have you settled bill?
Guest: No. I'd like to do that now.
Receptionist: You can settle your bill at the Finance Department on the fourth floor.
Guest: Okay. I've paid my bill.
Receptionist: Would you like some help with your luggage?
Guest: I think I can do it myself if I can borrow your trolley.
Receptionist: Certainly. Just a moment, please. I'll get it for you.

Conversation 2:
Cashier: Finance Department.
Guest: Hello, this is Mr. Lister in room 3406. I'll be leaving early tomorrow morning. So I'd like to come down sometime today to settle my bill.
Cashier: Very good. We are here until 8:00. We will have to disconnect your IDD line at 5:30 this afternoon, so it would probably be more convenient for you to settle your bill after 5:30 if you have any overseas calls you need to make today.
Guest: Okay. I'll come down around 7:30 then, is that okay?
Cashier: That's fine. We'll have your bill ready.
Guest: Hello. I'm Mr. Lister from room 3406.
Cashier: Good evening, Mr. Lister. We have your bill ready, here you are. That will be the total, it is 436 yuan.
Guest: Okay. Here you are.
Cashier: (counts it) Four hundred and fifty yuan. Here's your change. Please check it. And here's

	your receipt. Please remember to turn in your room key to the receptionist.
Guest:	I will. Goodbye.
Cashier:	Goodbye, Mr. Lister. We hope to see you again.
Guest:	Thank you. Bye now.

Useful expressions about check-in and check-out

What kind of room would you like (or prefer)?

Do you want a single room or a double room?

Would you like a room with bath or shower?

How long do you plan to stay here?

For how many nights?

How many people are there in your party?

I can book you a single room with shower for the 26th.

What time will you be arriving?

Unfortunately, we are fully booked for the 21st.

We won't be able to guarantee you a room for May 6th.

For a single room the price would be 35 dollars.

There is a small charge of 25 cents a day extra.

There's a reduction for children.

We'll extend the reservation for you.

You may keep the room till 3 p.m, if you wish.

III. AIRLINE RESERVATION

Read the following conversation between the caller and the reservation clerk.

Reservation clerk:	Northwest Airways, good morning. May I help you?
Caller:	Yes, I'd like to reserve a flight to L.A. for the first of October.
Reservation clerk:	One moment, please... Yes. There's a flight at 8:30 and one at 10:00. Let me check whether there're seats available. I'm sorry we are all booked up on that day.
Caller:	Then, any alternatives?
Reservation clerk:	The next available flight is Flight 812 at 8:30 Tuesday morning October 3. Shall I book you a seat?
Caller:	What about the fare?
Reservation clerk:	Economy, business class or first class ticket?

Caller:	Economy, please.
Reservation clerk:	That would be $176.
Caller:	Ok I will take the 8:30 flight on Tuesday.
Reservation clerk:	A seat on Flight 812 to L.A. 8:30 Tuesday morning. Is it all right, sir?
Caller:	Right.
Reservation clerk:	Could I have your name and telephone number, please?
Caller:	My name is Tony Jones, that's T-O-N-Y J-O-N-E-S. You can reach me at 536299.
Reservation clerk:	I will notify you if there is cancellation.
Caller:	Thank you for your nice service.
Reservation clerk:	Thank you for flying with us. Hope you have a nice trip.

Useful expressions about airline reservation

I'd like to change this ticket to the first class.

I'd like two seats on today's Northwest Flight 7 to Detroit, please.

I'd like a refund on this ticket.

The flight number is AK708 on September 5th.

There's a ten thirty flight in the morning.

I'd like to reconfirm my flight from London to Tokyo.

My reservation number is 2991.

Do you have any tickets available for that date?

Would you please make my reservation to Chicago for tomorrow?

What's the fare to New York, Economy Class?

Where do I pick up the ticket?

Can I have a second-class one way ticket to Chicago, please?

What time does the plane take off?

IV. RELEVANT LANGUAGES

Titles

Are you Mrs. Best?

You must be Professor Ford.

May I know your name, sir(madam)?

Here's a letter for you, Dr White.

You're wanted on the phone, Captain Smith.

Welcome to our hotel, miss Henry.

May I be of service to you, Mr. Baker?
Can I help you, Ms Blake?
Would you take the seat, young lady?

Self—Introduction

I'm Henry. I'm from Golden Lake Hotel. I'm here to meet you.
My name is Irene. I'm the housekeeping Department waiter.
I'm the receptionist here. Welcome to our hotel.
Reservations. May I help you?
Room service. May I come in?
This is Henry Adams speaking.

Offering Help

May I help you?
Can I help you?
What can I do for you?
May I take your baggage for you?
May I help you with your suitcase?
Would you like me to call a taxi for you?

Expressing welcome

Welcome, sir/madam.
Welcome to our hotel, sir/madam.
Welcome to our western restaurant.
We're glad to have you here.
I'm always at your service, sir/madam.

Unit 9 Business Travel

V. PRACTICING

1. Match the statements or questions (1–8) to the responses (a–h).

1. Good morning. Can I help you?	a. That's for the drinks you ordered from your room.
2. May I know your name and your room number, please?	b. Yes, that's all.
3. May I have your room key, please?	c. Yes. I would like to check out.
4. What's the 20 Yuan for?	d. Yes. I will.
5. May I help you with your suitcases, sir?	e. Dennis black, Room 1108.
6. How would you like to pay?	f. Thank you.
7. Do you have any baggage in the trunk?	g. Sure. Here you are.
8. It's slippery, please mind your step.	h. In cash. Here is the money.

2. Put the following conversation in the correct order.

Cashier

a. I'll see what we have, madam. Oh, yes. I can offer you a room on the eighth floor.

b. Thank you, Here is your key. It's Room 808 on the eighth floor.

c. Have you made a reservation?

d. May I see your passport?

e. Good afternoon, madam. Can I help you?

f. How long do you want to stay?

g. Thank you. Madam. Could you fill in this form, please?

Guest

h. No, I haven't.

i. Fine.

j. Thank you very much. Good night.

k. Good afternoon, I want a single room, please.

l. Three days.

m. Of course. Here you are.

n. Yes. Here it is.

The correct order:

VI. OPTIONAL READING

Business Travel

Business travel is the practice of people traveling for purposes related to their work. It is on the rise especially with foreign business markets opening up. 432 million business trips were completed by United States residents in 2009, which accounted for approximately $215 billion dollars towards the economy.

Many airlines began to concentrate on providing premium service on long haul flights especially for the first and business class business travelers with the development of more sophisticated business traveler needs over the last 15 years.

American Airlines was the first airline to offer a frequent flier program to customers. The Advantage program began in May 1981 and included Hertz car rental and Hyatt hotel. The first hotel to start an independent hotel program was Holiday Inn; they began in January 1983. National Car Rental was the first car rental company to introduce a program back in March 1987. Airlines have also been working on tools that benefit the business travelers such as: Improved and competitive mileage programs, quick check in and online check in, lounges with broadband connection, etc. Hotels are not far behind. They are also on the competition for the business travelers by offering flexible points programs, broadband connection in all rooms and fast check in and check out services.

While internet booking engines have become the first destination for around 60% of leisure travelers, business travelers, especially with the need for itineraries that may include more than one destination, have still found that a knowledgeable travel agent may be their best resource for better ticket pricing, less hassle and better air and land travel planning. For larger business travel accounts these travel agents take on a travel management role, and are referred to as Travel Management Companies (TMCs), providing services such as consultancy, traveler tracking, data and negotiation assistance and policy advice.

Recent trends in this market have extended to the implementation of Self Booking Tools (SBTs) which allow automated booking of trips within company policy, an increase in the inclusion of Duty of care practices in the booking and monitoring process and more consideration for the environmental impact of business travel.

Unit 10 Catering

Unit Aims

- To know how to reserve a table and receive guests
- To know how to take orders and serve dishes
- To master the basic expressions about catering
- To know some cultural background knowledge about catering

Warming Up

Ruth is a reservation clerk in a big restaurant. And she is preparing a list of English phrases to help her on the phone. What other phrases can you add to the list?

Good morning, Sir.
What can I do for you?
May I have your name, Sir?

1. TABLE RESERVATION

Read the following telephone call between a waiter and a reservation clerk.

Caller: Hello. Is this Robin Restaurant?
Clerk: Yes. Can I help you?
Caller: Yes, I'd like to reserve a table for tonight, please.
Clerk: Certainly, sir. How many people in all, please?
Caller: Nine.
Clerk: At what time can we expect you?
Caller: Oh, at 7:00 tonight.
Clerk: Just a moment, please. I'll check the availability for you. I'm afraid we're fully booked for that time. Is it possible for you to change the time?
Caller: Err... What about 8 o'clock?
Clerk: Certainly, sir. Would you like a table in the hall or in a private room, sir?
Caller: A private room, please.
Clerk: A private room for nine at 8 tonight. May I have your name and telephone number, please?
Caller: Sure. It's James Lee and my number is 556767.
Clerk: Thank you very much, Mr. Lee. We look forward to seeing you.
Caller: See you tonight. Goodbye.
Clerk: Goodbye.

1. Now write the message that Ruth takes.

Message

Number of people:
Lobby or private room:
Time of arrival:
Name:
Telephone/room number:

Unit 10   Catering

2. Put the following conversation in the correct order.

Customer

a. Five.

b. Oh, I see. I'd like it. My guests are all vegetarians.

c. May I have a private room?

d. At 7 o'clock this afternoon. Is it OK?

e. John Smith.

f. Yes. Do you have any vacant seats this afternoon?

g. what do you mean by special service?

Waiter

h. And then, when are you coming?

i. I mean for veggie lovers or something the like.

j. Yes, there're still some available. Are you ready for a reservation?

k. Mr. Smith, how many guests are there in total?

l. Hello! China Hotel. Can I help you?

m. Yes. I'll arrange that for you in time. Your name, please?

n. OK. Do you need any special service?

Useful expressions about table reservation

How many are there in your party, Sir?

A deposit of $30 is required to secure your booking.

And can I stand a chance of getting a table by the window?

Any special requirement?

I'm sorry, we're not open on Saturdays.

I'm afraid that table is reserved for 8 p.m.

II. RECEIVING THE GUEST IN THE RESTAURANT

Read the following telephone call between a waiter and a customer.

Waiter: Good evening, sir and madam. Welcome to our restaurant. Do you have a reservation, sir?

Customer: I'm afraid not. Do you have a table for three?

Waiter: I'm sorry to say that we haven't got any vacant seat at present. Now would you please take a seat and wait over there? We can seat you in ten minutes or so.

Customer: It sounds nice. Sara, let's go there then.

(Ten minutes later)

Waiter: I'm sorry to have kept you waiting so long, sir and madam. Now we have a table for you. Could you please come with me, please?

Customer: May we have the table by the window?

Waiter: Oh, that table has been reserved.

Customer: It's a pity.

Waiter: Well, what about the one that is further back but still offers a view of the lake?

Customer: OK. I'll listen to you.

Waiter: Would you like a high chair for your child?

Customer: Yes, please.

Match the statements or questions (1–8) to the responses (a–h).

1. Do you have a reservation?
2. Do you have a table for two?
3. Where would you like to sit?
4. Good morning. Two persons?
5. What would you like to order?
6. Are you ready to order?
7. Anything else, sir?
8. How would you like your steak, sir?

a. Yes, two, please.
b. We'd like to try some Chinese snacks.
c. Yes, we do. A reservation for two under Smith.
d. We would like a table by the window.
e. I'm sorry to say that we haven't got any vacant seat at present.
f. No, thank you! That's all for now.
g. I'll have it well-done, please.
h. Yes. We want to eat Chinese food.

Unit 10   Catering

Useful expressions about receiving guests

Good evening, sir. Welcome to our restaurant.
Have a good evening.
This way, please.
We have a window table reserved for you.
We can seat you very soon.
Would you mind moving over a little?
Would you please wait in the lounge for about five minutes?
I'll seat you if the table is ready.

III. TAKING ORDERS

Read the following telephone call between a waitress and a customer.

Waitress:	Good evening, sir and madam. Welcome to our restaurant. Have you made a reservation?
Customer:	No, we haven't.
Waitress:	A table for two?
Customer:	Right.
Waitress:	This way, please. Would you like to take this table?
Customer:	It's fine.
Waitress:	Take your seat, please. Are you ready to order now, sir?
Customer:	For an appetizer, smoked salmon.
Waitress:	And, for the main course?
Customer:	A T-bone steak and a rump steak.
Waitress:	Why not try the roast pork? It's the specialty of our restaurant.
Customer:	No, thanks. I have to avoid food containing too much fat.
Waitress:	Would you like it rare, medium, or well-done?
Customer:	Well-done. And we'd like two salads and two hamburgers.
Waitress:	What kind of vegetables would you like?
Customer:	The curried vegetables.
Waitress:	What soup would you like?

Customer:	Mushroom soup.
Waitress:	What do you want for dessert?
Customer:	Two ice-creams.
Waitress:	Any more requests?
Customer:	No, I'm afraid that's all.

Useful expressions about taking orders

Shall I make a recommendation?
May I take your order now?
Would you like to order now?
What have you decided on?
I'd like to try the chicken, please.
Is there a set menu for lunch?
Your dish takes ten minutes to prepare.
What will you have to follow the soup?
I'm sorry, there are no chops left.
We have both buffet-style and a la carte dishes, which would you prefer?
Do you have today's chef's dish?

IV. SERVING DISHES

Read the following telephone call between a waiter and a customer.

Waiter:	Your roast Beijing Duck.
Customer:	Ah, it looks good. Can you tell me how to eat it?
Waiter:	Yes, please wrap the Beijing duck in the pancake with the spring onion and the sweet bean sauce. You'll find the taste's better.
Customer:	I'll have a try. (*Tastes*) Hm, good indeed.
Waiter:	Your fried shrimp balls.
Customer:	Shrimp! Are you sure there's a shrimp inside? It doesn't look like it!
Waiter:	Please have a try, madam. And you'll see the shrimp.
Customer:	Hm, what's the seasoning made from?
Waiter:	It's mixture of pepper and various spices. It should be sprinkled on your food.
Customer:	I see. Thanks.

Waiter:	This is the soup you ordered, madam. Shall I put it in the middle of the table?
Customer:	Yes, please.
Waiter:	This is the complete course. There is the dessert to follow.

(After ten minutes, he brings the dessert.)

This is your dumplings. Please put a little vinegar on the plate and dip them into it before eating.

Customer:	OK. It's really delicious.
Waiter:	How about something to drink?
Customer:	No, I think that's enough for me. Thank you for your service.
Waiter:	You're welcome, madam. Take your time and enjoy it.

Useful expressions about serving dishes

Please enjoy your dinner.
Here's the fried shelled shrimp. (Is it) yours?
Would you hurry up?
Did you enjoy your meal?
Your fried chicken, sir. Where shall I put it?
Watch out for the plate. It's a little hot.
Please hold the food, we still have one friend coming.
I'm really sorry about that. I'll tell the chef to hurry.

V. CATERING LANGUAGES

Table reservation

We are open from 6 in the morning to 11 in the evening.
We serve 24 hours.
We are open round the clock.
Can you give me your name, please?
For how many?
Who's the reservation for?

Receiving the guest

Would you mind sitting here in the corner?
You can sit where you like.
Where would you like to sit?
Is this table suitable?
I'm sorry, there aren't any tables left now.

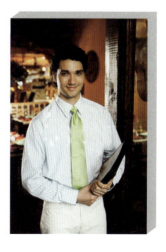

I'm sorry, the restaurant is full now.
Have you been served?
Please step this way.

Taking orders
Are you ready to order?
What would you like to start with?
What would you like to follow?
Everything is a la carte.
We have a buffet. You can have all you want for $ 10.
I suggest you have a taste of Sichuan dishes.
I'd recommend this dish to you.
It's delicious and worth a try.
Do you care for a dessert?

Serving dishes
Could I serve you anything else?
If you need anything else, just feel free to tell me.
I do apologize for giving you the wrong dish.
I seem to have misserved a dish.
What's the problem, sir?
I'll take it to the chef and see what he can do.
How would you like your eggs?

VI. OPTIONAL READING

Table Reservation

When the guests ask you to reserve for him, you must pay more attention to ask him to the table or private room. Ask the guest about the information of the table reservation: the number of the persons; a table in the lobby or a private room is needed by the guests; the demands for the table or the private room; the time of arrival; under whose name the reservation is made; and the contact telephone number or the room number. Then confirm and express your expectation to the guests.

Unit 10 Catering

Receiving the Guest in the Restaurant

Ask the guests if they have a reservation or not. If "yes", lead them to the booked table. If "no", ask them the number of people, and escort them to choose a table that fits them.

When the guests are going to seat, arrange them take their seats as soon as possible. Pour the tea or some drinks immediately. Lead the guest to the toilet. And ask them to wait a moment.

After the guests are seated, give them the menu.

Taking orders

The order of the western dishes begins from the host or hostess generally. If the host wants the guests order by themselves, begin from the first guest (by the right to the host or hostess). Usually, men order for the women. The ladies don't order.

Receiving the order begins from counterclockwise. And remember the cover code of the guest. So the waiters can serve the dishes correctly.

Pay more attention to asking the guest about his demands in detail of the order when you take the order. So the chef can cook by his demand.

After the guest ordered the food or beverage, the waiter should read the meal the guest ordered one by one.

Serving Dishes

After the guests almost have arrived, you can ask them politely: " Excuses me, may I serve you?"

Before serving dishes, call the correct name of the dish. "Hello, this is ..., please enjoy!" If the dish is the specialty, you should give the introduction and illustration.

If the guests need to divide the dishes, at first, you should ask them: "Would you need to divide your dishes?"

After serving the last dish, you should be in a whisper to tell the guests: "This is the complete course."